Enchantment of the World

THE PHILIPPINES

By Emilie U. Lepthien

Consultants: Leonard Casper, Ph.D., Boston College, Chestnut Hill, Massachusetts

Stephen Burke, Undergraduate Asian Studies, University of Michigan, Ann Arbor

Consultant for Social Studies: Donald W. Nylin, Ph.D., Assistant Superintendent for Instruction, Aurora West Public Schools, Aurora, Illinois

Consultant for Reading: Robert L. Hillerich, Ph.D., Bowling Green State University, Bowling Green, Ohio

CHILDRENS PRESS, CHICAGO

A typical rural home

This book is dedicated to the Tablantes—
Esther Fe, Nat Jr., and Jose and their
wonderful parents, Isabel and the late
Dr. Nathaniel Tablante, and to so many
other Filipino friends

Library of Congress Cataloging in Publication Data

Lepthien, Emilie U. (Emilie Utteg)
  The Philippines (Islas Pilipinas)

  (Enchantment of the world)
  Includes index.
  Summary: Presents an overview of this Southeast
Asian nation of 7107 islands.
    1.   Philippines—Juvenile literature.
[1.   Philippines]   I.   Title.   II.   Series.
DS655.L43   1984   959.9   83-23152
ISBN 0-516-02782-4   AACR2

Picture Acknowledgments
Philippine Office of Tourism: Cover, pages 14 (2 photos),
21 (right), 26 (bottom), 73 (right), 81, 86 (bottom right), 92
(left), 93 (left, top and bottom), 109
©**Milt and Joan Mann/Hillstrom Stock Photos:** Pages 4, 5,
18 (left), 19, 20 (left), 47, 62 (right), 66, 69, 97, 111, 124
©**Jack Lund/Hillstrom Stock Photos:** Pages 6, 38, 45, 51
(left), 94 (top), 102 (top right), 106
©**Byron Crader/Root Resources:** Pages 51 (right), 68
(right)
Emilie U. Lepthien: Pages 8, 10, 17, 20 (right), 25, 26 (top),
31 (2 photos), 32, 34, 35, 37, 40, 42 (2 photos), 44, 48 (top),
57, 61, 68 (left), 71, 73 (left), 74, 76 (top), 79 (right), 82
(2 photos), 84, 86 (top), 90, 92 (right), 99, 102 (top left and
bottom)
National Archives: Page 11
Gladys J. Peterson: Pages 16, 18 (right), 65, 94 (bottom)
©**James Stenning Rasin/Hillstrom Stock Photos:** Pages 21
(left), 55, 76 (bottom)
©**Grace H. Lanctot/Root Resources:** Pages 23, 62 (left), 79
(left)
Len W. Meents: Maps on pages 16, 25, 48, 49
Bruce L. Cook: Page 93 (right)
©**Fred Livingston, Jr./Hillstrom Stock Photos:** Page 53
**The International Rice Research Institute, Laguna,
Philippines:** Page 58
**Courtesy Flag Research Center, Winchester,
Massachusetts 01890:** Flag on back cover
Cover: Rice terraces in Mountain Province

Rural children often accompany their mother when she does the laundry.

TABLE OF CONTENTS

Children from a rural grammar school on Luzon

Chapter 1

THE PHILIPPINES—
ISLAND NATION

The Republic of the Philippines has been called an Island Nation, Pearl of the Orient, the Friendly Islands, and the New Society. All of these terms describe this archipelago of more than seven thousand islands. They form an arc between the South China Sea and the Philippine Sea and Pacific Ocean beyond.

THE COUNTRY WITH MANY NAMES

The Philippines is known as the Pearl of the Orient for several reasons. Off the coast of Mindanao oysters are gathered for their pearls. The country has been called a "pearl of great price" for the beauty of its mountainous islands, the priceless qualities of gentleness and loyalty of its people, and the rich resources of its land.

It is also a nation of friends, the Friendly Islands. No people could be more hospitable than the Filipinos. They are friends of people everywhere.

The Philippine archipelago stretches from north to south off the coast of Southeast Asia. The islands form a chain between Taiwan

Fishing boats and an inter-island freighter at Zamboanga

on the north and Malaysia and Borneo on the south. Only 688 miles (1,107 kilometers) across at its widest part, the country lies in the tropics. The climate is warm and humid in the lowlands, cooler in the mountains.

There are almost five hundred ports and harbors. They have been excellent stopovers for ships sailing between Australia and Japan and those en route to other Asian and Indonesian destinations. Many ports provide safe anchors when typhoons lash the islands.

The republic has an oceangoing merchant fleet, but its inter-island fleet also is extremely important. Coastal vessels carry passengers and freight between the islands.

THE NEW SOCIETY

The New Society refers to the form of parliamentary government that replaced the Philippine congressional system derived from the American constitution. It refers, too, to the expanding economy, foreign trade, industrialization, increased agricultural production, and foreign relations.

In September 1972, President Ferdinand Marcos proclaimed martial law throughout the country. He termed it the beginning of a "New Society." Major reforms were to take place in seven areas: law and order, land holdings, labor, the economy, education, social services, and government.

The country experienced many changes in the years following. But problems remain and solutions are difficult to find.

THE FILIPINOS

Some scientists believe the islands may have been inhabited for 250,000 years. Others believe the first arrivals were dark-skinned pygmies called Negritos who crossed on land bridges from Asia about thirty thousand years ago.

The great majority of Filipinos are descendants of Malays who came by boat before the Christian era. Later, Indonesians, Chinese, Arabs, Spaniards, and finally Americans settled on the islands. The ethnic background of many Filipinos is often a combination of at least two nationalities.

Today there are two official languages: Pilipino (derived from Tagalog), and English. Eighty-seven different native languages are spoken on the islands. Until recently, people on different islands had difficulty understanding each other.

A statue of Lapu-lapu, chief of the Mactan during the time of Magellan, stands on Mactan Island.

FOUR PERIODS OF HISTORY

Philippine history can be divided into four periods. From the time of the first settlers on the islands until the Spanish arrived, communities were scattered and ruled by chieftains. The first migrations had been over land bridges during the last glacial period. Later migrations were over water. This was the first period in Philippine history.

The Spanish period began when Ferdinand Magellan landed, first on some of the smaller islands, and finally on Cebu on March 16, 1521. He claimed the islands for Spain.

In succeeding years other Spanish ships visited the islands. In 1542 the archipelago was named Islas Filipinas in honor of Prince Felipe, later Philip II of Spain.

Commodore George Dewey

The first permanent Spanish settlement with a fort and church was established on Cebu in 1565. Spain ruled the islands as a colony until 1898.

Toward the end of the nineteenth century, Filipinos sought independence. The Philippine Revolution began in 1896. During the Spanish-American War of 1898, Commodore George Dewey led an American fleet into Manila Bay, where on May 1, 1898, the Spanish fleet was destroyed. On June 12, 1898, the Filipinos celebrated national independence. But the third period in their history was just beginning. They found themselves under American colonial administration.

The Filipinos expected the United States to recognize their independence. Before long, fighting broke out between American occupation forces and Filipino republican forces. Many Americans thought the Filipinos should have independence. Others, however, felt it was wiser to keep the islands as a colony.

Finally, in 1916, the United States assured the people complete independence once a stable government was established. In 1936 when the Philippines became a commonwealth, they were assured of independence in 1946.

However, on December 8, 1941, the Japanese attacked the Philippines. By May 1942, the Japanese were in control. Three years later American soldiers aided by Filipino guerrillas regained the islands.

The fourth period in history began on July 4, 1946, when the commonwealth became the Republic of the Philippines.

PROBLEMS OF THE NEW REPUBLIC

Only Warsaw, Poland suffered worse destruction than Manila in World War II. Food shortages, malaria, cholera, poverty, graft, and lack of funds were tremendous problems faced by the new democracy after the war. Lawlessness increased due to guerrilla activities. One guerrilla group, the Huks, had strong Communist ties. The Muslims (Moros) resented having inadequate representation in the Christian government, along with resettlement of Christians on Muslim lands in the south.

Many problems still exist. The population is growing rapidly. More than half of the fifty million people are below the age of twenty. At least 600,000 new jobs must be created each year to employ those reaching working age.

Land reforms are still necessary. Many tenant farmers have very low incomes. Owners are entitled to a large share of crop harvests.

Housing, sanitation, transportation, and communication demand improvement. More electrical power is necessary for industrial and home use. Investment capital is needed to increase industrial development.

There are unresolved conflicts between the majority of the people, who share a common culture and religion, and minority groups. These minorities include the Muslim Filipinos (Moros) of Mindanao and the Sulu Archipelago, scattered groups of "pagans," and the Chinese on the islands.

THE FUTURE HOLDS PROMISE

For centuries the Filipinos have faced difficult challenges. Those that confront the people and the government today are very great. Nevertheless, with a growing pride in their own nation, Filipinos have taken their place in international organizations such as the United Nations. Ties to the United States are strong. Economic relations benefit both countries.

Natural resources are abundant. Major agricultural crops—rice, sugar, coconuts—are produced in sufficient quantities to permit export. The seas around the islands abound in edible fish. The fishing industry is expanding.

There are vast deposits of copper, nickel, iron, silver, gold, and chromite. Oil wells off Palawan may reduce dependence on foreign supplies. Manufacturing and industrial production are increasing yearly.

These beautiful islands with their warm and friendly people have become, in many ways, a model for other countries in Southeast Asia. The government places great emphasis on education for both children and adults.

"Mabuhay!" (may BOO high) is how Filipinos greet visitors. It is a warm greeting. "Mabuhay" they say in farewell. It is a fond farewell with the hope they will see you again. "Mabuhay" says much about the people of a country "where Asia wears a smile."

The Hundred Islands (above), rich in marine life and coral gardens, lie off
the west coast of Luzon in the Lingayan Gulf. With their sandy beaches they are
ideal for tourism, whereas the rugged coastline (below) is not.

Chapter 2

THE CHANGING LAND

THE ISLANDS ARE FORMED

Scientists believe that thousands of years ago there were land connections between Borneo and what are now the Philippine Islands. They believe that plant and animal life, as well as people, traveled over these land bridges.

Following the Ice Age, the sea level rose as the ice melted. The ocean covered low-lying areas, creating islands where there had been land.

Scientists also believe that great upward thrusts of the ocean floor, together with volcanic action, formed some of the thousands of islands. They have found coral formations a mile (1.6 kilometers) above sea level in the mountains of northern Luzon. Sixty-five percent of the total landmass of the island is mountainous.

Today small islands continue to rise out of the sea through volcanic action. Some islands can be seen only during low tide. Only 154 islands exceed five square miles (thirteen square kilometers) in area. Over 2,000 of the 7,107 islands have not been named and fewer than 1,000 are inhabited. Only 11 islands are of economic importance.

Small coral islands

THE SEAS AROUND

For 1,100 miles (1,770 kilometers) the archipelago forms a barrier between the Pacific and Indian oceans. In 870 miles (1,400 kilometers) only two major seaways open the islands to the Pacific. One is the San Bernardino Strait between Luzon and Samar. The other, the Surigao Strait, lies between Leyte and Mindanao. Ships must pass through small internal seas after sailing through these straits. During World War II Allied and Japanese fleets fought to control these two routes.

Mayon Volcano on Luzon erupted in September 1984 and 45,000 people were evacuated.

In the Pacific Ocean east of Mindanao lies the deepest section of any world ocean. The depth has been measured at 6.7 miles (10.8 kilometers or 5,900 fathoms). In the South China Sea, between mainland Asia and the islands, the sea is relatively shallow. The calm waters, except during typhoons, provide safe inter-island sailing routes.

In the cooler months, monsoon winds arrive from the northeast. From April to October the monsoons blow from the southwest. They carry heavy rains, especially from July through October. During these months an average of twenty typhoons strike the islands.

Earthquakes, volcanic eruptions, and typhoons continue to change the land. Upheavals expose rich mineral deposits. Volcanic activity, although destructive, enriches the soil with ash. Seasonal rainfall in the northern islands and local rainfall outside the typhoon belt support diverse crops.

Because of the warm climate, rice and orchids thrive.

A TROPICAL SETTING

The Philippines lies within the tropics. The climate in the lowlands is warm and humid. The average temperature is 80 degrees Fahrenheit (27 degrees Celsius) year-round. In the mountains it is much cooler.

On Luzon, the average annual rainfall ranges from 35 to 216 inches (89 to 549 centimeters) depending upon the location. The wet season on Luzon lasts from June to November. Although many of the islands experience cyclonic storms or typhoons, only a few storms cause great destruction and flooding with severe crop losses.

The soils on the islands are more fertile than those in most other tropical areas. Limestone formed from coral, the skeletons of tiny marine animals, contributes to soil fertility. Ash from volcanic eruptions has also created fertile soil. Unfortunately,

This wood-carver has his raw material in his yard.

erosion caused by heavy rains washed tons of fertile topsoil down to the sea each year. Nonetheless, many plains have been built up along the coastline by these alluvial deposits. Agriculture flourishes on these plains.

More than ten thousand different species of flowering plants and ferns grow throughout the islands. There are over a thousand species of orchids. Evergreen forests can be found in the lowland areas and up to 2,000 feet (610 meters) on the mountainsides where there is sufficient rainfall. There, too, the native Philippine mahoganies grow to enormous size. Where there are distinct wet and dry seasons the molave (hardwood) forests can be found. Molave trees belong to the teak family.

Narra is the national tree. For a week in March or April its long showy clusters of yellow flowers bring beauty to the streets of cities where it is planted. Its hard wood is used in manufacturing furniture and for wood carvings. Narra is found in lowland rain forest regions.

Coconuts ready for processing (left), and a field of pineapple plants (right)

Mangrove swamps line the coast. Its unusual root system supports the mangrove tree in high as well as low tides. Mangrove trees supply firewood for the stoves and ovens of coastal villages.

The coconut is called the "Tree of Life" in the Philippines. Traditionally, Filipino families planted a coconut tree at the birth of a child. Although coconuts may float on the sea, wash ashore, and grow, most coconut palms are raised on plantations or small farms. Coconut palms are seldom found at altitudes above 1,000 feet (305 meters).

There are many other interesting native plants, including bamboo, bananas, cassava, and pineapples. Many of the plants have come from Malaysia, Indonesia, and even Australia.

A papaya tree (left), and a tarsier, a small nocturnal mammal (right)

Almost eight hundred species of birds have been identified on the islands. Of these, one hundred species are migratory. There are few wild animals. Monkeys, small deer, wild pigs, and some members of the cat family can be found in more remote areas. There are dozens of kinds of rodents, plus fifty species of bats. Crocodiles were once numerous throughout the islands but now exist mainly in Mindanao. There are some poisonous snakes.

Over 750 species of saltwater fish are caught for food. The warm seas around the islands abound in fish, mollusks, and pearl oysters.

THE GEOGRAPHIC DIVISIONS

Although the archipelago is generally divided into three major geographic divisions, people also define three smaller divisions. These regions or divisions are determined by the proximity of the islands. They are not based on physical, agricultural, or social similarities.

The Luzon or northern region includes the largest island, Luzon. It has one third of the nation's total land area, 40,420 square miles (104,692 square kilometers). The main part of the island is 250 miles (402 kilometers) long and between 75 and 100 miles (121 and 161 kilometers) wide. A long peninsula stretches to the southeast.

Three mountain ranges on the island run almost parallel in a north-south direction. In northern Luzon the Sierra Madre range is very close to the Pacific shore. It leaves very little coastal lowland. The Cordillera Central is in the west. The two ranges are separated by the Cagayan Valley, a rich agricultural region 140 miles (225 kilometers) long and 40 miles (64 kilometers) wide.

The Zambales Mountains stretch from the Lingayan Gulf south to Manila Bay. They hug the shores of the South China Sea, leaving a narrow coastal lowland. The Central Luzon Plain lies below the Cordillera Central. It is the country's most important agricultural area, 100 miles (160 kilometers) long and 50 miles (80 kilometers) wide. Manila Bay on the west coast is one of the finest natural harbors in the world. Manila is located on its eastern shore.

The long peninsula of southeastern Luzon is a mountainous volcanic area. Heavy rainfall and the fertile volcanic soil make over one half of the peninsula agriculturally productive.

Rice terraces in Mountain Province, northern Luzon

The Luzon group includes many small islands to the north. Amianan Island is only 200 miles (322 kilometers) south of Taiwan.

South of Batangas Province on Luzon is Mindoro Island, seventh largest in the country. It is considered a frontier area. Although its population is small, as Luzon becomes crowded more people are moving to Mindoro. Some persons include the island in the Luzon group, while others consider it a subdivision together with numerous smaller nearby islands. Mindoro is very mountainous with peaks that rise about 8,000 feet (2,438 meters).

Another smaller division is Palawan, fifth in size. A long narrow island (275 miles; 442 kilometers), it stretches southwest below Mindoro. Very likely it was once part of a land bridge from Borneo. Over 1,100 islands and islets surround it. The island is sparsely populated. However, its forests have several important commercial species of trees. Oil has been discovered off the northern Palawan coast.

Between Luzon and Mindanao is the second major group, the Visayan Islands, or Visayas. This group includes over half of the Philippines' 7,107 islands. There are seven large islands including Samar, the country's third largest. Samar and Leyte act as a buffer against storms originating in the Pacific Ocean. The two are linked by the longest man-made bridge in Southeast Asia, 1.36 miles (2.2 kilometers) long.

All seven islands—Cebu, Negros, Panay, Samar, Leyte, Bohol, and Masbate—are important agriculturally. Corn, rice, abaca (hemp), and coconuts are the principal crops. Sugar is grown extensively on Negros. The largest sugarcane mill and refinery in the world is located at Bacolod on Negros.

Cebu is the center for corn cultivation. It also has the country's largest copper mine and produces coal and limestone for cement. It is one of the country's most prosperous islands and the most heavily populated.

South of the Visayas is Mindanao, the second largest island. Together with small islands around it, Mindanao forms the third major group. Its rugged mountains and extinct volcanic peaks are cloaked in forest of great commercial value. Mount Apo, highest peak in the Philippines (9,692 feet; 2,954 meters) is a dormant volcano. The island's large central plateau is the site of cattle ranches and pineapple plantations. Rubber, coconuts, and abaca are raised in the lowlands.

The cities of Zamboanga on the southwestern tip of Mindanao, Davao in the southeast, plus the coastal areas (particularly in the south) have a large concentration of Muslims. Crescent-topped minarets can be seen from great distances.

The third of the smaller divisions, sometimes included with Mindanao, is the Sulu Archipelago. This chain of eight hundred

Abaca fibers, used in making rope, dry in the sun near Davao, Mindanao.

small coral and volcanic islands (five hundred unnamed) stretches from Zamboanga Peninsula for 200 miles (322 kilometers) toward Malaysia. Many of the islands are heavily forested. Fishing is an important industry. The people are able to raise enough food for their own use.

SIMILAR BUT DIFFERENT

Islands in each geographic group are related by their nearness to each other. However, they differ in physical, social, and economic conditions. Many factors contribute to the type of activities in which the people engage. These factors include the calm waters of the inter-island seas, climatic differences, soil fertility, and the type of coastline.

Most of the people have a Malayan heritage that dates back for two thousand years or more. There are other ethnic groups represented, too. Differences in language and in religious beliefs are sometimes divisive. Nevertheless there is a strong sense of national unity.

Malays, Indonesians, Chinese, Arabs, Spaniards, and Americans settled in the Philippines. Many Filipinos often are a combination of at least two nationalities.

Chapter 3

A NATION OF MANY PEOPLE

Filipinos have a legend about the origin of their people. Long ago, the legend tells, the Creator took clay and fashioned two figures. He put them into an oven to bake. When he took them out they were too pale. They became the race of Westerners. He tried again. But this pair he left in the oven too long. They were very dark. They become the people of Africa. The third set was baked just right. Their color was a warm, golden brown. The Creator had fashioned the Filipinos.

Legends are interesting but scientists search for accurate answers. They have tried to determine Filipino origins. Some believe the islands may have been inhabited 250,000 years ago. However, they have been unable to find proof of this. In the Tabon caves of Palawan, a long slender island stretching southwest from Mindoro, they have found evidence of early habitation by Stone Age people.

THE NEGRITOS

These Stone Age people, the Aetas or Negritos, came from mainland Southeast Asia over land bridges about thirty thousand years ago. The Negritos were dark-skinned pygmies standing only 4 to 5 feet (1.2 to 1.5 meters) tall.

Fewer than 25,000 Negritos still live in the jungles of northern Luzon, Palawan, and Mindanao. They are skillful hunters and food gatherers. Some of the men have taught American pilots, soldiers, sailors, and marines these skills at the Jungle Environmental Survival Training School at the United States naval base at Subic Bay.

THE TASADAYS

A small tribe of just twenty-five persons was found in the mountains of Mindanao in 1971. These Stone Age people are called Tasadays. They are food gatherers. Their diet consists of fruits, bamboo and rattan shoots, and crabs found in forest streams. Untouched by the outside world, they knew nothing about iron or steel. Their main shelter is in caves reached after a very rugged climb. They, too, build lean-tos, but only for temporary shelter.

PRESERVING MINORITY CULTURE

The Tasadays and other mountain tribes live in areas where loggers, farmers, and miners frequently seek more land. President Ferdinand Marcos appointed Manuel Elizalde, Jr., as presidential assistant for national minorities to assist tribes in maintaining their own cultures. He also headed PANAMIN, the Private Association of National Minorities.

It was PANAMIN that first contacted the Tasadays. Worldwide interest in this Stone Age tribe benefited other cultural minorities.

There are more than sixty different groups living in remote regions on several islands. They retain their ancient, traditional life-styles. Some still do little farming. The Ifugao of northern Luzon, however, are exceptions.

Minority population numbers about four million. The president stated that minorities wishing to be integrated into Filipino life could do so. But the rights of those who preferred to maintain their original ways of life would be protected. A 300,000 acre (121,410 hectare) municipality has been established on Mindanao for 175,000 tribal members.

In 1972 a 50,000 acre (20,235 hectare) reserve was established to protect the Tasadays and another tribe. Outside exploitation is forbidden. Loggers and miners cannot enter, lease, or purchase any part of the reserve.

The members of many tribal groups are descendants of the Proto-Malays. These people probably arrived from Indonesia in two waves, 5,000 and 3,500 years ago.

MALAY ORIGINS

The vast majority of Filipinos are of Malay origin. The Malays arrived in more recent times. Their culture became the basis of Filipino life today. They came in small sailboats called *barangays.* When several families formed a village they called it a barangay. The Spanish changed that to *barrio.* In 1974 the old term, barangay, was again used, but often in referring to city districts or even neighborhood units.

The Malay settlers were expert fishermen, seamen, and farmers. Even today their descendants living in the lowlands near the sea continue as both farmers and fishermen.

OTHER CULTURES, OTHER PEOPLE

Among other people coming to the islands were Chinese traders. Some stayed and set up trading communities. Chinese have been in the Philippines since the tenth century. By the fifteenth century the Japanese were also engaged in trading.

Hindus, Indonesians, and Arab traders had come even earlier. Islam, the religion brought by Arabs and Indonesians, spread from the Sulu Archipelago to Palawan and Mindanao. The followers of Islam are called Muslims. They number about four million.

Since 1975 the Muslims have sought a separate country formed from Mindanao, Palawan, and the Sulu Archipelago, as well as part of Sabah in Malaysia. The Philippine government has claimed Sabah under a nineteenth century grant from the Sultan of Sulu. Muslim relations with the national government and the Christians on the southern islands are still strained.

On the islands themselves migration continued for centuries. The Negritos were driven from the lowlands into the mountains by the Proto-Malays from Indonesia. Today there has been integration among all of the groups except for the Muslims and small tribes in the mountains.

HOUSING

In rural areas, houses are still built as they were four hundred years ago. Huts of bamboo and wood are raised above the ground on wooden pillars. They are roofed with nipa fronds from a type of palm. Nipa huts usually have only one or perhaps two rooms, which are reached by a ladder. Except in rainy weather, cooking is

A nipa hut on Luzon (left), and new construction in metropolitan Manila

done outdoors. Charcoal or wood heats the stoves. Nipa huts are quickly and easily constructed. In high winds they are often destroyed.

In Banaue, the rice terrace region of northern Luzon, the Ifugao build nipa huts with large wooden washers on the bamboo pole supports. These prevent rats from climbing the poles. At night chickens are placed in wicker coops that hang from the raised floors.

In the cities, of course, houses are built of more permanent materials. They are larger, too. Often they have lovely little gardens behind fences. Some sections, like Forbes Park near the Manila American Cemetery outside Manila, have large compounds where people of great wealth live.

Makati, one of the large towns included in metropolitan Manila, is the new business center. Large, expensive apartments are for rent or for sale as condominiums. There are also exclusive private homes and new large hotels.

31

The cross Magellan planted in 1521 is encased in a shrine in Cebu.

Chapter 4

THE LONG ARM OF
HISTORY

Philippine history can be divided into four periods. The first is the longest. It began when the Aetas or Negritos came across land bridges from Indonesia, Borneo, and Sumatra. They were followed centuries later by those who sailed the barangays. Although traders came from many parts of the Far East, no country made an attempt at colonizing. All this changed with the beginning of the second period—the Spanish arrival in 1521.

THE SPANISH PERIOD

The population of the islands may have numbered 500,000 when Ferdinand Magellan arrived. In 1493 Pope Alexander VI had issued a decree. It assigned all past and future discoveries of land some distance west of the Azores to Spain. Discoveries east of the line were to be claimed by Portugal. Magellan, a Portuguese navigator, wanted to sail west. But the king of Portugal refused to support a voyage to find the Spice Islands of the East Indies by sailing westward. So Magellan sought and received backing from Spain.

An aerial view of Cebu today

Magellan commanded five ships that left Spain on September 20, 1519. When he reached Samar, an island in the Visayas, in March 1521, only three ships were left. Magellan named the islands the Archipelago of San Lazaro (St. Lazarus) because they were sighted on that saint's day. On Easter Sunday he landed on Limasawa near Leyte. Following a religious service, Magellan claimed the islands for Spain.

A Limasawa chief guided the Spaniards to Cebu. Even then Cebu was a busy port. Traders and merchants came from the East Indies, China, and Siam (Thailand). Magellan planted a cross on Cebu when he landed. The chief, Rajah Humabon, was friendly. Soon he and his wife and many of his people were baptized and converted to Christianity.

Magellan offered to help Humabon in his battle with Lapu-lapu, chief of Mactan, a small island across a narrow strait from Cebu. Magellan landed on Mactan with a small force. He and eight of his men were killed. The others retreated and the two

Inside this basilica on Cebu is an image of the Holy Child brought by Magellan.

ships now left in the small fleet sailed quickly from Cebu. Finally one ship reached Seville, Spain, on September 6, 1522. It had been an incredible journey — the first voyage around the world.

For a quarter of a century Spain sent other squadrons to control the islands. In 1542 an expedition landed on an island the men named "Felipina" in honor of Spain's crown prince. Soon the entire island chain was called "Islas Filipinas." Today, Filipinos use "Republika ng Pilipinas" as their country's name.

Miguel Legazpi set sail from New Spain, as Mexico was then called, in November 1564. He was headed for the Philippines. Spain was anxious to colonize the islands and to spread Christianity. It also wanted to control the sea route to the Spice Islands and to make contacts with China and Japan.

Legazpi landed on Cebu and established the first Spanish settlement. A fort and church were quickly built. For six years Legazpi and his men struggled to survive. There was a shortage of food. Then in 1568 a Portuguese fleet arrived.

Actually, the Philippines lay on the Portuguese side of the pope's line of demarcation of 1493. The Portuguese commander demanded that the Spanish leave. When Legazpi refused, the Portuguese bombarded the settlement, blockaded the port, and set fire to the rice fields. For three months the Spanish resisted. Then suddenly the attackers left. Legazpi remained in control.

The Spanish decided to find a safer location than Cebu. They moved to Panay, an island northwest of Cebu. Panay had a better food supply and could be defended more easily.

From Moro Muslim traders Legazpi heard of a town with a good harbor farther north on the island of Luzon. Legazpi's grandson found the town. It was Maynila, the northernmost base of the Muslims.

Legazpi sailed from Panay for Maynila. He defeated Rajah Sulayman and the Muslims. They retreated south to Mindanao. Legazpi ordered the remaining Filipinos to complete a fort they had started building. The fort was at the mouth of the Pasig River. Later, Fort Santiago, a stone fortress, was constructed where the original stockade had stood. It took 149 years to complete. The fort was badly damaged at the close of World War II, but is a national monument today.

Manila, as it soon was spelled, became the seat of Spanish rule on the islands. Trade between Manila and Mexico brought wealth to Spain. Silks, porcelain, and tea from China, cottons and carpets from India, spices from Indonesia, and gems from Ceylon (Sri Lanka) were shipped via Manila to Mexico. Silver was returned in Spanish galleons. The galleons were constructed of strong molave wood in shipyards in Cavite near Manila. Filipino laborers were poorly paid and Filipino seamen were often impressed into service on the ships.

Fort Pilar, built in 1635 as a Spanish lookout on Cebu, now is a shrine of the miraculous image of Our Lady of the Pillar.

The islands were not without other European invaders. Sir Francis Drake, an Englishman, landed on Mindanao in 1577. Ten years later another English ship tried to capture a shipyard on Iloilo. At sea, English ships fought the Spanish galleons. The British also wanted to establish colonies on the islands.

The Dutch had long sought a route to the East Indies. When Spanish, Portuguese, Chinese, and Japanese ships approached the Philippines, the Dutch attacked them. Several times between 1609 and 1648 the Dutch blockaded Manila harbor. However, they were never able to capture the city. When the Dutch took possession of the Molucca Islands to the south, they ended their attempts to occupy the Philippines.

In 1762 the British returned. They captured Manila. For a year and a half the British flag flew over the city. When the Seven Years' War in Europe ended in 1763, the Treaty of Paris restored Manila to Spain.

*Fort Santiago
in Intramuros*

The Filipinos had seen, however, that the Spanish were not invincible. The Spaniards, in turn, realized they needed additional protection.

Legazpi had built a Spanish-style city inside a wooden stockade. Soon thick, stone walls protected the town, Intramuros ("within the walls"). A moat around the walls and drawbridges at the seven gates to Intramuros offered further protection.

Inside, the walled city had narrow streets, stone houses, and a central square. Around the square were government buildings, a church, schools, houses, and Fort Santiago. The governor-general's palace stood proudly as a symbol of Spanish rule. Filipinos and Chinese had to live outside the walls.

In 1863 an earthquake destroyed the palace. At the outset of World War II, the Japanese bombed Intramuros. But the greatest damage came when the Americans retook the city in 1945. The Japanese in Manila made their last stand in Intramuros. Today the walls are being rebuilt. But most of the elaborate churches are lost forever.

SPANISH INFLUENCE IN FILIPINO LIFE

When Magellan landed, many of the Filipinos used a writing system borrowed from the Hindu or Javanese. Many spoke their own languages—and still do. Few attempts were made to teach the Spanish language. Even after three hundred years of Spanish rule, less then 10 percent of the population was allowed to learn the language.

One of Spain's main objectives was to spread Christianity. Many Roman Catholic priests were sent to convert the people. The Spanish erected churches throughout the islands. Today, the Republic of the Philippines is the only Christian country in all of Asia.

The Filipinos had seen that the Spanish could be defeated when the British captured Manila. The people longed for independence. There were many uprisings around the country.

The great majority of the people were extremely poor. A medieval economic arrangement was introduced by the Spanish. The king allotted large grants of unoccupied land to Spanish officers or to the church. Each landowner, in turn, was to govern the people in his territory and defend them. The people paid tribute to the landowners, either in money or crops.

The Filipinos also were taxed by Spain, the local community, and the church. Men between sixteen and sixty years of age had to work forty days a year on public projects without pay.

Street cleaners rehearsing for the Independence Day parade

No Filipino could hold any office higher than chief of a village or barangay. Chiefs paid no taxes but were expected to collect them from the village residents.

All of the people were expected to live "under the bells"— within the sound of church bells. Priests started hundreds of barangays. The first building constructed was usually the church. There was a close relationship between the church and the government. The priests became the most important persons in the barangays. In a country of so many islands, the church became the unifying agent.

For many years there was no serious threat to Spanish rule. Finally, toward the end of the nineteenth century, a united uprising and revolution occurred. The result was a declaration of Philippine independence on June 12, 1898. The second period in Philippine history was almost over.

Chapter 5

INDEPENDENCE—BUT WHEN?

Under the Spanish, the population remained mostly rural. Very few Filipinos benefited from the Spanish galleon trade with Mexico. Filipino men built the galleons and served as sailors on them, but the pay was meager. Little was done to improve the economic or social level of the people.

In 1872 Filipino workers and troops at the Cavite arsenal mutinied. They sought better pay and working conditions. The uprising was quickly quelled. Three Filipino priests who sought equality with Spanish priests were arrested. They were executed near Manila Bay in what is now Rizal Park. They became martyrs in the nationalistic cause.

FILIPINO PATRIOTS

A new group of Filipinos began to emerge. Educated in Europe and the United States, they were doctors, lawyers, and other professionals. They became leaders in the nationalistic movement. They were called *ilustrados*—the enlightened ones.

The most famous Filipino patriot is Dr. Jose Rizal. He was a

The building in Fort Santiago where Dr. Rizal was held before his execution (left). "My Last Farewell" is inscribed in Spanish and Tagalog on the tomb of Rizal (right).

man of integrity who realized there was a great need for reform. Rizal had been abroad. When he returned home he joined a society working to correct injustices. He was arrested as a revolutionary although he had not advocated revolution. He was sent into exile in northern Mindanao. His writings were banned.

Andres Bonifacio formed a secret society known as KKK. Its name was taken from three Tagalog words—*Kilusang Kanuhayan at Kaularan*—meaning Society of the Sons of the People. The Katipunan, as the society was called, believed that revolution was the only way to achieve independence. Bonifacio asked for Rizal's help, offering to free him from exile. But Rizal refused.

The Spanish returned Rizal to Manila where he was imprisoned in Fort Santiago. On August 25, 1898, Bonifacio led his men against Spanish troops, the first skirmish in the revolution. The revolt spread rapidly.

Rizal's trial began in November. He denied he had supported the revolution. Nevertheless, the Spanish sentenced him to death.

Jose Rizal was a respected doctor, artist, and author. His writings touched his people deeply. The night before his execution he wrote a beautiful poem, "My Last Farewell." It began, "Land that I love, farewell: O land the sun loves: Pearl in the sea of the Orient. . . " Early in the morning of December 30, 1896, he faced a firing squad. His death united the people and increased their desire for freedom.

General Emilio Aguinaldo took over command of the Filipino army. A constitution was drafted and Aguinaldo was elected president in November 1897. Within a month Aguinaldo signed a truce with the Spanish, expecting reforms. He and his followers went into exile in Hong Kong.

Like the Philippines, Cuba was still under Spanish rule. In April 1898, the Spanish-American War broke out. While American troops went to Cuba's aid, Commodore George Dewey commanded an American fleet that sailed into Manila Bay on May 1, 1898. Battles were fought between Spanish and Fil-American forces. By mid-August the Spanish surrendered Manila.

Commodore Dewey had encouraged Aguinaldo to return. On June 12, 1898, the Filipinos declared national independence and General Aguinaldo returned as president. With the end of Spanish control the people felt certain the United States would recognize their action.

They were soon disappointed. The Treaty of Paris officially ended the Spanish-American War on December 10, 1898. Cuba had its independence, but the Spanish ceded the Philippines to the United States. The Philippine-American War broke out.

The home of Emilio Aguinaldo in Cavite Province, Luzon. In spite of American claims to the territory, Aguinaldo was elected the first president of the Philippines January 23, 1899.

Aguinaldo insisted that his country's independence be recognized. When the war ended in 1902, the United States was in control.

Civil service and courts systems were established. Military rule was ended. Church and state were separated. Although these reforms were accepted, the people still longed for independence.

The Jones Law of 1916 promised independence whenever a stable government would be established. Three branches of government were formed. The executive branch was headed by a governor-general appointed by the president of the United States.

COMMONWEALTH OF THE PHILIPPINES

The Philippines received commonwealth status in 1935. In national elections Manuel Quezon was elected president and

After the Japanese landed on Manila, General MacArthur left. This statue shows him returning to Leyte in 1944 accompanied by President Osmeña.

Sergio Osmeña, vice-president. Complete independence was assured by 1946.

General Douglas MacArthur was sent to the islands, where he had served previously. He was to build a defense force for the new government. American forces were still stationed on the islands. The Japanese attacked on December 8, 1941. Their planes bombed American army, air force, and naval bases with devastating effects in the first few days of the war in the Pacific.

WORLD WAR II

Japanese ground troops landed north and south of Manila. On January 2, 1942, they entered the city. American and Filipino troops fought valiantly for several months. MacArthur and his headquarters staff moved to the island of Corregidor. President Quezon, Vice-president Osmeña, and their staff joined them. Fil-

American troops were already stationed on this fortified island at the entrance to Manila Bay.

As the situation became more desperate, America's President Franklin D. Roosevelt ordered MacArthur to leave for Australia. President Quezon and his government officials were urged to set up a government-in-exile in the United States.

On May 7, 1942, the Philippines were surrendered. The Japanese had taken over the islands.

Japanese occupation was very unpopular. Underground and guerrilla activity increased. Over half a million Filipinos joined in these activities.

MacARTHUR RETURNS

When he left, General MacArthur vowed to return to the Philippines. On October 20, 1944, following a landing of American troops on Leyte, he waded ashore. He had returned. He was accompanied by President Osmeña, who had assumed the office upon the death of President Quezon a few months earlier. Japanese resistance on the islands continued until the final surrender on September 3, 1945.

A fierce battle had been waged in Manila. The Japanese destroyed much of the city as they retreated and further damage was done by the liberation forces. Manila lay in ruins.

THE REPUBLIC OF THE PHILIPPINES

The task of rebuilding was enormous. In less than a year the country was scheduled to attain complete independence. Elections were to be held in November 1945. So many problems faced the

Bitter fighting occurred on Corregidor, which is an island at the entrance to Manila Bay, between the Japanese and the Filipino and United States troops. A Pacific War Memorial has been erected on the battlefield.

people that elections were postponed until April 1946. The economy was devastated. Disease, shortage of water, lack of adequate power, and a government divided between those in exile and those who served under the Japanese were deterrents to forming a new government.

Nevertheless, Manuel Roxas was elected the first president. On July 4, 1946, he was inaugurated. The Stars and Stripes were lowered and the flag of the Republic of the Philippines was raised.

Manila harbor is the busiest port in the Philippines (above). The "Ring of Fire" (below), a narrow band of volcanic and earthquake activity, follows the Pacific coast. Mayon Volcano last erupted in 1968 and Taal in 1965.

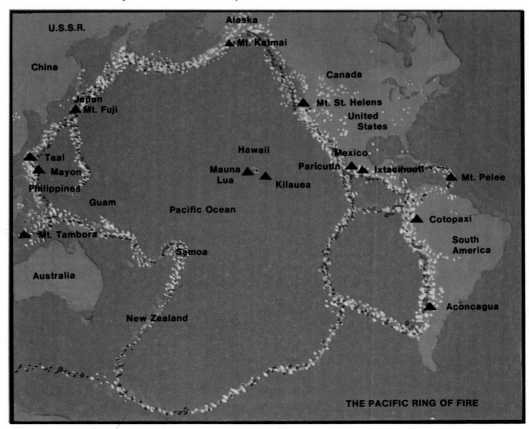

THE PACIFIC RING OF FIRE

Chapter 6

TRAVEL AND COMMUNICATION

Fewer than 1,000 of the 7,107 islands in the Philippine archipelago are inhabited. Most economic development has taken place on the eleven largest islands. The topography of the islands has greatly influenced their development.

The islands lie in what has been called the "Ring of Fire." This ring is a narrow band of intense volcanic and earthquake activity that follows the Pacific coast. It includes North and South America, New Zealand, Indonesia, the Philippines, eastern China, and Japan.

There are ten active volcanoes in the Philippines and many more dormant ones. Volcanic activity and earthquakes have shaped the islands, leaving them mountainous and with irregular coastlines. But sixty natural harbors have provided safe anchorages for inter-island ships for centuries and have enabled commerce with other countries to flourish.

Manila Bay is one of the world's finest harbors. Its 770-square-mile (1,994-square-kilometer) area helps it to compete with Hong

Kong and Singapore as an international shipping center. Manila's strategic location on air routes to and from the Far East helps to draw international conventions. Opened in 1976, the Philippines International Convention Center is an imposing structure built on reclaimed land in Manila Bay.

TRANSPORTATION BY SEA

The first people who migrated to the islands used barangays (boats). Inter-island ships continue to be the best means of transporting goods from one island to another. Passengers, too, rely on these ships, since the cost of airplane tickets is often prohibitive.

Seventy percent of foreign imports arrive in Manila and must be reloaded on inter-island ships for transport to other islands. The national government operates 80 ports. Another 390 ports are under the jurisdiction of municipalities. Sugar mills or centrals, pineapple and coconut growers, flour mills, and petroleum importers have their own piers and wharves.

Foreign goods may be off-loaded only at national ports. The government has registered 156 inter-island vessels and 130 oceangoing ships. The Philippine merchant fleet sails to ports around the world. Ships under foreign flags also maintain regular service to the Philippines. Dozens of foreign freighters can be seen in South Harbor in Manila Bay every day.

Domestic trade is also carried on by boats stopping at river towns. Some of these boats are poled or rowed; others are motorized. The Pasig River flows through Manila. It is short but very important commercially, connecting the Philippines' largest freshwater lake, Laguna de Bay, with Manila Bay.

Barge traffic on the Pasig River (left). A Muslim vinta with its colorful sails (right)

The Cagayan and Pampanga rivers in northern Luzon also carry many riverboats. In the dry season the Abra River is busy with bamboo rafts loaded at Cagayan and poled upstream.

On Mindanao two rivers, each 200 miles (322 kilometers) long, are important commercially. The Mindanao empties into the Moro Gulf near Cotabato, an important seaport. The Cotabato Valley has great agricultural potential and crops such as corn are taken downstream to the seaport. The Agusan empties into the Mindanao Sea near Butuan. Near this seaport city thousands of porcelain and jewelry artifacts dating back to the Ming and Ching dynasties in China have been unearthed.

Ferries carry both goods and passengers between islands that are close to each other. Sometimes *vintas*, boats with long outriggers, provide ferry service.

The Muslims are expert shipbuilders. They build vintas primarily for fishing, but they also construct larger vessels. In

Zamboanga the port is a major focus of daily activity. Ferry and cargo vessels vie for space at the docks with long, enclosed motorboats called *kumpits.*

THE PAN-PHILIPPINE HIGHWAY

The more than seven thousand islands stretch 1,100 miles (1,770 kilometers) from north to south and span as much as 668 miles (1,107 kilometers) from east to west. Bridges connecting all the islands would be impossible to construct. Nevertheless, the most important road is the Pan-Philippine or Maharlika Highway. It was completed in 1980. Its many sections run from Cagayan in northern Luzon for 1,250 miles (2,011 kilometers) to Davao in southern Mindanao. The longest section is on Luzon, passing through Baguio, Manila, and Legaspi and ending at Matnog on the San Bernardino Strait.

Trucks, buses, and cars must cross the strait on ferries to Samar Island. Farther south, the San Juanico Bridge, the longest in southeast Asia (1.36 miles; 2.2 kilometers), connects Samar with Leyte.

Ferries operate across Surigao Strait so that vehicles can reach Mindanao. The highway traverses twenty-one provinces and passes through eleven cities and many barangays or barrios. It is an important route for commerce and passenger service.

ROADS, TRUCKS, CARS, AND JEEPNEYS

Only 18 percent of the nation's roads are paved with concrete or asphalt. Many of the paved roads are not serviceable throughout the year. Feeder roads are important to provide low-cost farm-to-

Jeepneys in Manila

market transportation. Recognizing this need, the government has undertaken an ambitious highway-improvement program.

There are almost 900,000 motor vehicles in the country. Half of these are cars. Sometimes, in rush hours, it seems that every vehicle in the country must be on the streets of Manila. To move people more rapidly and with less congestion, an elevated light rail system is under construction in Manila. Expressways north and south of Manila have been extended.

At the end of World War II, hundreds of jeeps remained on the islands. These were quickly converted into small buses. They became an important inexpensive mode of transportation in the cities.

Jeepneys, as these small buses were called, became so popular that when they wore out new and larger jeepneys were built to replace them. Passengers enter at the rear. Benches are located on both sides. In rush hours jeepneys are very crowded. They operate on specified routes that are painted on the sides. The newest jeepneys are vividly painted and decorated with silver-colored horses or many rearview mirrors mounted on the hood. Often they carry a saint's name. The fourteen thousand jeepneys in Manila increase traffic congestion and contribute to air pollution.

RAILROADS

Building and maintaining railroads on the islands are very costly. National railroads have been constructed only on Luzon and Panay. Philippine National Railways now operates 643 miles (1,035 kilometers) of main line and 625 miles (1,006 kilometers) of branch lines and sidings between San Fernando in La Union Province north of Manila, down to Legaspi near the southeastern end of Luzon. Tracks are often washed out by typhoons.

On Panay there are only 73 miles (117 kilometers) of track, operated by the Philippine Railroad Company. Nevertheless, rail lines are important to farmers as a means of inexpensive transportation for their products.

Some sugar mills or centrals and logging companies operate their own short-haul lines. The private lines carry products to company ports.

THE AIRLINES

Government-owned Philippine Air Lines (PAL) operates flights between Manila and cities in Europe, Asia, Australia, and the United States. On the islands are five international airports. Manila's new international terminal building is modern and

Carabao are important to the farmers.

convenient. The second most important international terminal is on Mactan Island. A new highway and bridge connect Mactan with Cebu.

Domestic flights to fifty cities are also on PAL's schedule. The number of inter-island flights is increasing and domestic air freight also has increased.

In two hours passengers can fly from Manila to Cebu (Mactan). From there they can continue to Zamboanga or Davao in other short flights. Inter-island ships may take several days for such trips.

BEAST OF BURDEN

Carabao or water buffalo are an important means of transportation in rural areas. Farmers ride these patient animals to rice fields and then use them for plowing or to pull heavy loads on sledges.

The carabao has thick horns that curve back toward the shoulders. Its hide is thick and almost hairless. It must wallow in mud or water to soften its hide and to keep insects off. Its broad splayed feet enable it to walk through the muddy rice paddies.

CARRYING MESSAGES

For many years after the telephone was introduced on the islands, communication was limited to each island. Modern technology has improved the system. Two main telephone systems now serve the country. The government-owned system serves cities through the Bureau of Telecommunications. Privately owned Philippine Long Distance Telephone Company has over forty-eight telephone exchanges and operates throughout the country.

MASS COMMUNICATIONS

Radio broadcasting in the Philippines began in 1922. Broadcasting facilities destroyed during World War II were rebuilt with modern equipment. Now there are over 270 commercial and noncommercial stations. However, many rural people still cannot afford radios and must rely on information passed on by word of mouth.

Through relay stations television programs reach homes not only in Manila but in other urban areas. Half of the registered families in Manila own television sets. The national ownership is about 5 percent.

Control room of a radio station in Baguio

THE PRINTED WORD

Following independence, Filipinos took great pride in their free national press. The number and ownership of newspapers was limited during martial law from 1972 until 1981. Major publications, such as the *Manila Times,* the *Manila Chronicle,* and the *Philippines Free Press,* remained suspended after martial law was lifted. Many other cities and provinces have daily or weekly publications. Daily business newspapers and publications cover industrial and professional needs. There are also more than twenty popular weekly magazines.

Harvesting rice by hand

Chapter 7

FOOD FOR A HARDWORKING NATION

Fifty-nine percent of the land is forested and 31 percent is under agricultural production. There are areas too rugged for cultivation. Some areas have poor soil and lack water resources.

Fortunately, varied climatic conditions enable farmers in different regions to raise both tropical and temperate zone crops. Agriculture is the basic industry of the country.

RICE—STAPLE FOOD

Rice is not only the main agricultural product but also the principal food crop of the population. At least 75 percent of the people consume rice daily. One fourth of the population depends upon the rice industry for some kind of employment.

More than 40 percent of the cultivated land area is planted in rice. Although it can be grown throughout the islands, there are three major rice-producing regions. They are the central plain of Luzon, Panay and Negros in the Visayas, the Catabato and Lanao regions of Mindanao.

Like many other countries in Southeast Asia, the Philippines until recently was not self-sufficient in rice production. The annual yield could not meet the demands of an ever increasing population. Then, in 1967, "miracle rice" was introduced. It was developed after seven years of crossbreeding at the International Rice Research Institute (IRRI) located at the College of Agriculture of the University of the Philippines, at Los Banos outside Manila. Students at the university often work in the experimental program at the institute. In 1961 only three countries participated in the institute's work. Now thirty-four countries send trainees.

Hundreds of types of rice and hybrid rice are planted and tested for resistance to pests and disease and, most important, for increased yield in a shorter growing period. Some types of rice grow best in irrigated fields. Others must be improved for dry land, shallow, deep-water, and floating rice areas. Floating rice areas have fields that are flooded to at least a yard (one meter) in depth during typhoons.

Despite a rapidly increasing population, the Philippines has been able to supply its own needs and export a surplus of new rice strains. However, when drought, such as the country experienced in 1983, or typhoons hit, exports are reduced.

Most farmers have used carabao or water buffalo for work in rice paddies for centuries. Mechanized equipment would make the work of plowing, planting, transplanting, tilling, fertilizing, and harvesting much easier. However, farms are small and such equipment is expensive.

In the mountains of northern Luzon, the Ifugao tribe grows rice on terraces. Through careful irrigation and farming they have prevented soil erosion on their 14,000 miles (22,526 kilometers) of terraces.

Farmers winnowing rice

Elsewhere, soil erosion is a major problem. The most fertile soils
are found on the plains and in valleys, usually near the coast.
Much of the land has been cultivated for hundreds of years. In
areas previously not under cultivation, the method called slash-
and-burn is used to clear the land. This method, flooding, and
poor drainage all have resulted in soil erosion.

On Cebu in the Visayas, half of the arable land has lost 75
percent of its topsoil. Areas on Luzon, Bohol, and Masbate are also
badly eroded.

Erosion prevention has a high priority in the program of the
National Pollution Control Commission. Soil erosion has been
responsible for the near extinction of some native plants and
animals. The National Soil Erosion Management Committee
assists farmers in proper land management. Farmers are taught
terracing, contour farming, the building of diversion canals, and
grass waterway planting.

Drying corn and grains (left) and a fruit market (right)

CORN

Corn, the second most important staple food is raised primarily in the Visayas and on Mindanao.

Failure to rotate crops, double and triple cropping on steep hillsides, and improper contour plowing have caused erosion. As a result the soil requires great quantities of fertilizer.

The government offers farmers a subsidy and buys much of the corn crop. In storage, unfortunately, corn weevils destroy part of it.

"PLANT FOR LIFE"

The "Plant for Life" campaign in the Green Revolution project has resulted in many small gardens and vegetable plots. The Filipino diet is often deficient in proper nutrition. This is as much the result of ignorance of basic nutritional practices as of widespread poverty or lack of land. The government encourages the planting of a type of squash called sayote, sweet potatoes, yams, cassava roots, and other root crops and vegetables for home use and sale in markets.

ABUNDANT FRUITS

A wide variety of fruits can be found growing around many homes and for sale at roadside markets. Fruits include bananas, pineapples, papayas, citrus fruits, and mangoes. Bananas grow throughout the islands. The many varieties range from small ladyfingers to large Sabas used for cooking. About half of the banana crop is exported. Large refrigerated banana freighters can be seen in Davao Gulf. Japan imports most of the crop destined for foreign markets.

One third of the country's pineapples, fresh or canned, are consumed on the islands. The rest is shipped to other countries. Pineapple canning is one of the few large-scale food processing industries along with sugar and coconuts. Two thirds of the pineapple exports are canned.

COFFEE AND CACAO

Coffee plantations can be found above the 1,000-foot (305-meter) level on the uplands of Batangas Province of Luzon, south of Manila Bay, and on the mountainsides of Mindanao.

Cacao, from which cocoa and other chocolate products are derived, is raised in the same regions as coffee. It also grows well on southern islands in the Sulu Archipelago and in the Cagayan Valley in northern Luzon.

SUGAR

The major export commodity is sugar, refined or partially refined. Cane fields provide work for farmers, refinery workers, and people engaged in transportation. The sixteen sugar centrals (mills) on the Visayan island of Negros produce 61 percent of the nation's sugar. Victorias Milling Company at Bacolod is the largest integrated sugarcane mill and refinery in the world.

Harvesting is done from December to May. The cane must be transported quickly to the mill or it will lose its recoverable sugar content. At the mill the cane is cut automatically, washed, and crushed. The juice from the stalks is then processed to separate the raw crystalline sugar from molasses. The raw or brown crystalline sugar can be processed or refined to provide white crystals.

COCONUT PRODUCTS

Siamese junks carried traders for coconuts long before Magellan arrived. Today coconut products are the third most important export, surpassed only by sugar and semiconductor devices. The islands are the world's largest producer of coconuts and products derived from them: copra, dessicated or shedded coconut, and coconut oil. The oil is used in many countries to make margarine, soap, detergents, plastics, candy bars, and cake frostings.

Every part of the coconut palm is useful. No wonder it is called the "Tree of Life." The branches can be used for shelter, the nectar of the flowers to provide a sweet drink, the nuts for food and drink, the husks for many useful products, and finally the trunk for lumber.

Coconut palms grow to a height of one hundred feet (thirty

A coconut palm

meters). A single tree may produce as many as two hundred nuts a year near the crown. The average, however, is about thirty nuts.

An expert climber scrambles up a tree, his bare feet fitting into notches in the trunk. With a sharp knife, often at the end of a pole, the climber cuts off the nuts. They fall to the ground cushioned by the thick husks. Green coconuts are cut thirty days after the fruit begins to form. The thirst quenching liquid inside is called water.

The outer husk is removed by piercing it with a sharp spike. The husk provides a strawlike material used in making brushes, sacks, fishing nets, rope, insulating products, and wallboard.

The white meat inside the husk is dried. This results in copra, which is sent to the oil mill to extract the oil. The remaining pulverized copra is used as animal feed or fertilizer.

Coconut palms grow throughout the islands on small farms. Plantations are found on Luzon, on the Visayan Islands of Cebu, Leyte, Samar, and Albay, and on Mindanao. The crop may be floated to market on coconut rafts or ferried from small islands to ports such as Davao.

Fish market in Malabon, north of Manila

Chapter 8

RESOURCES UNLIMITED

Although much of the country suffers from typhoons and torrential rains and most islands are mountainous, natural resources are abundant. These include grasslands, forests, minerals, and over two thousand species of fish in salt and fresh waters.

FISH AND FISHERIES

The islands lie in a fertile fishing belt. The traditional Filipino diet consists of rice and fish. Fish and fish products are a major source of protein.

The coastline of the more than seven thousand islands has a combined length of 10,000 miles (16,090 kilometers). In September 1979, the Philippines extended its maritime jurisdiction to the 200-mile (322-kilometer) Exclusive Economic Zone. This added 193,045 square miles (500,000 square kilometers) of territorial waters. About 16 percent of the total zone is now included as coastal waters and the rest is open sea.

Fishing resources are found in three areas: ponds and fresh water, inshore (coastal), and deep sea. The coastal waters are the

Drying fish (left) and a young coral seller (right)

most productive. Mangrove swamps along the shores and coral reefs bring nutrients to these waters. At least fifty-two large fishing grounds are frequented by commercial fishermen.

Fifteen percent of the marine fish production occurs in the coral reefs. Coral has been collected for construction and ornaments. Since nearly one half of the reefs are now in poor condition, a ban has been placed on the export and trading of coral.

About thirty thousand men on motorized vessels carry on commerical deep-sea fishing. They utilize trawl lines, gill nets, and purse seines. Tuna are caught in large quantities. Canned tuna is a product of the Philippines. The total export of fish and fish products in 1980 was over $107,000,000 in United States funds.

Anchovies, sardines, herring, mackerel, grouper, sea bass, and snappers make up the major fresh fish market. Some fish are salted to preserve them while others are dried in the sun.

Most of the commercial catch is landed in the Manila area. Other fishing ports are located on Masbate, Cebu, Samar, Negros, Panay, and Cuyo.

The continental shelf around the islands is narrow. Many local fishermen operate in these municipally controlled waters. In some cases, fishermen drag nets or push a kind of seine as they wade

Fishing boats returning to the harbor

along the shore. Other fishermen have small outrigger crafts, from which only one or two persons may fish. Larger outriggers have crews of six or more men.

The fishing industry has not been developed to its maximum potential. This is due in part to a lack of new commercial vessels and adequate refrigeration and processing facilities.

Fish ponds and fish pens can be found in Lake Taal and Laguna de Bay near Manila, as well as in lakes in many other parts of the country.

In fish pens, bangus (milkfish), tilapia, and carp are "farmed." The pens are made of bamboo and nylon netting. Existing organisms in the water are used to feed the fish. Fish pens may be 26,900 square feet (2,500 square meters) in size and hold up to 12,500 fingerlings. The water can be drained from the ponds to harvest the fish. The fish are fed rice bran, small shrimp, and moss. Harvesting takes place six or seven months after the fingerlings are introduced into the ponds. The fish are sold immediately at local markets, where the demand is great.

Fingerlings of dalag (mudfish) are introduced into the water of rice paddies between crops, then harvested when fully grown. In addition to the income from the fish, this method helps to fertilize the paddies.

THE GRASSLANDS

Although fish is important in the Filipino diet, there is a lack of adequate animal protein. To improve nutrition, the Bureau of Animal Industry has encouraged an increase in livestock and poultry industries. There are an estimated 12,350,000 acres (499,045 hectares) of grasslands. Some are of low productivity. Others are rangelands and grazing lands. Some of the grazing lands are in mining areas or are being developed for human settlement.

The government program to improve the quality of the grasses and legumes on rangelands is essential. This program will increase the number of livestock that can be supported on the rangelands.

A growing portion of the grasslands has been exposed to environmental hazards through population expansion and poor farming practices. Grass fires have also reduced the area of good pasturelands. Farmers and livestock owners sometimes start fires in summer, hoping there will be fresh shoots for animal feed during the rainy season.

LIVESTOCK

Before the Spaniards arrived, Filipinos were raising domestic animals—carabao, hogs, and goats. The wealth of a man was measured by the number of animals he owned.

Today's native cattle stock came from Mexico and China. Vast pasturelands exist on the islands in the Sulu Archipelago, and in provinces on Luzon, Mindanao, and Masbate. Over two million head of beef cattle are raised in these regions and on small farms

Plowing with a carabao

throughout the country. Carabao came from India or Ceylon and number more than five million. Although they are used as draft animals, they also provide meat and milk for the population. Dairy farms are found near Manila and a few other cities. Goats are also raised for meat and milk.

Swine or hogs are raised on farms of all sizes. Foreign breeds such as the Poland-China, Berkshire, and Duroc-Jersey have improved the quality. There are almost twelve million head of hogs.

Next to farming, the livestock industry employs the largest number of people. Modern slaughterhouses provide refrigerated facilities for cold storage of carcasses. Tanneries and fertilizer plants make use of animal by-products.

POULTRY

Poultry were introduced from Mexico by the Spaniards. Many rural families raise chickens and gather the eggs for family consumption and for sale. Commercial farms now assure a steady supply of eggs and chickens for urban areas. The country is now self-sufficient in poultry and egg production.

Duck raising is popular in towns bordering Laguna de Bay, where there is a supply of freshwater snails for feed. Both duck eggs and the slaughtered fowl are sold by farmers at local markets.

FORESTS AND FORESTRY

Mangrove forests are important. They protect and stabilize the coastal zone, reduce storm damage, and provide a habitat for fish and mollusks. They are also a source of timber, firewood, charcoal raw material, and tannin used in tanning leather and in dyes and inks.

Mangrove stands, as well as the nation's other forestlands, are being depleted through illegal cutting, agricultural expansion, and inadequate reforestation. This has resulted in soil erosion and flooding throughout the archipelago. Other problems result from deforestation, which alters patterns of rainfall, wind paths, and temperatures.

The Philippine forests are considered to be the most diversified in Southeast Asia. The government owns 97.5 percent of the forestland. Large commerical forests are found on Mindanao, Palawan, and Luzon.

Red lauan trees grow to great heights. Because of their huge diameters, they provide excellent lumber—the darkest colored

Mahogany logs are trucked down the mountains to sawmills (left). Tapping a rubber tree (right)

Philippine mahogany used in furniture manufacturing. Among other hardwoods the narra and molave are especially important. Molave is the most serviceable wood and the best furniture is made of narra.

Sawmills and processing plants produce lumber, veneers, and plywood. Timber and plywood are exported chiefly to the United States and Japan. Factories now produce paper pulp, paper, and cardboard in increasing quantities.

The Philippine tropical broad-leaved hardwoods and two species of pines are among the fastest disappearing forest resources in Southeast Asia. The government now bans the exportation of logs. This encourages conservation and the development of the local processing industry.

An abandoned gold mine near Baguio

MINERALS AND MINING

The country has extensive proven and potential reserves of metallic and nonmetallic minerals. Deposits of chromite, nickel, and copper are among the largest in the world. Gold, silver, iron, manganese, mercury, zinc, lead, cobalt, and uranium have also been mined.

Chromite mining declined considerably in 1981 due to high operating costs, a decline in steel making in other countries, and the mining of lower grade ores. Chromite is used to make iron and steel rustproof. It also increases the strength of steel. Zambales Province in western Luzon has reserves of millions of tons of the ore.

Copper has been the most important mineral for many years. Philippine copper production is the largest in the Far East. The principal mine, located at Toledo on Cebu Island, is worked through underground tunnels as well as by open pit. Other copper mines are found on Luzon, Negros, and Samar.

Gold mines can be found on Luzon near Baguio and on other islands as far south as Mindanao. In the 1970s the country was one of the top ten gold producers in the world.

Iron ore ranked after copper and gold in economic importance in the 1970s. Major deposits are found on Luzon, Mindanao, and the Visayan Islands. A mine on Camarines Norte was reopened in 1982 after six years' suspension.

Nickel mining and processing, an industry founded in 1975, handles 75 million pounds (35,020,000 kilograms) of nickel metal and alloy yearly on Nonoc Island off the northeastern coast of Mindanao.

Coal deposits have been found on Luzon, Mindoro, and Mindanao. The most significant coal mining, however, is carried on in southern Cebu.

In mid-1982 three oil wells off Palawan Island began producing five million barrels of oil annually. Additional oil fields have been located both offshore and on the islands. Domestic oil production is expected to provide almost 14 percent of the total petroleum requirements of the country by 1985.

A solar drier (above), is one of the many alternative energy projects. Food processed this way lasts twice as long as that air-dried in the sun. Water power can be used to produce energy (left).

Chapter 9

ENERGY, INDUSTRY, AND TRADE

As do other new nations, the Philippines for many years remained primarily an import country. Industrialization depends on many features, including capital investment, education, and constant source of energy.

Agriculture, the chief Philippine industry, alone cannot increase economic development. Philippine trade with industrialized and developing countries depends upon increased production at home. Energy, industry, and trade are interdependent.

THE ENERGY PLAN

In 1973 the republic paid $230 million for 68 million barrels of In 1981, 60.8 million barrels cost $2.6 billion—eleven times as much as eight years before. To reduce the amount of imported oil, the country embarked on an energy conservation program. By 2 imports were reduced by 4.4 million barrels. The reduced cost of oil also helped reduce the deficit in the balance of payments.

The country continues its efforts to develop alternative sources of energy. Coal, hydro power, wind power, solar energy, alcogas, bio-diesel, bagasse, and other nonconventional sources have been tried.

OIL AND COAL

The accelerated country's development of energy resources has reduced the country's dependence on imported oil to only 80 percent. Oil wells on an offshore basin in northwest Palawan produce a modest amount of oil. By 1987, 139 exploratory wells, two thirds offshore, will have been sunk. The saving to the country will amount to millions of dollars. It is expected that less than 40 percent of needed oil will have to be imported.

It is estimated that coal reserves are equal to six billion barrels of oil. The coal development program should displace oil in some energy intensive industries as well as in power generation. Although by 1987 over 4,400,000 tons (4,000,000 metric tonnes) will be mined, it still will be necessary to import coal. Philippine coal must be mixed with higher quality coal to provide the greatest benefits.

ALTERNATIVE ENERGY SOURCES

Nonoil sources will gradually decrease dependence on oil. Coal will provide 18.5 percent of energy sources; geothermal power, 14 percent; hydro power resources, 12.4 percent; nuclear energy, 4.8 percent; and alcogas, coco-diesel, and other nonconventional sources, 1.5 percent. Some of these alternative or nonconventional energy sources will enable farmers in the most remote regions to have electricity.

Geothermal power is being developed at an accelerated rate. There are at least fifteen sites where underground steam can be tapped to generate power. On Luzon two geothermal generating stations operate at Tiwi and Los Banos near Manila. Another field

ol extracted from sugarcane is one ingredient used in alcogas (left).
energy is used to evaporate crude salt from these beds near Manila (right).

eyte is operating with aid from New Zealand. The Philippines
econd only to the United States as producers of geothermal
er.

nuclear power plant has been under construction at Bataan.
ium deposits exist on the islands.

cogas, a nonconventional energy source, is made by
cting waterless alcohol from sugarcane, cassava, and other
ulture crops. It is blended with motor fuels.

the use of diesel fuel in vehicles increased, experiments to
d coconut oil with diesel were undertaken. The first coco-
l was sold in Manila in July 1982. The blend consisted of 97
nt diesel and 3 percent coconut oil. The mixture was
able shortly thereafter in provincial retail outlets. Coco-diesel
ld be more expensive per liter, as motor fuel is sold in the
ppines, but the government provides a subsidy. This permits
at no increase in price.

e refuse from crushed sugarcane stalks is called bagasse. The biofuel made from bagasse is used in sugar processing plants to generate power.

Biogas fuel, produced from decomposed agricultural wastes, is being used to provide energy in rural homes. The wastes include rice straw and hulls, and chicken, hog, and cow manure. Farmers are taught how to build biogas digesters. The waste from six hogs will provide enough biogas to meet the needs of the average Filipino family. The gas can be used to operate LPG (liquefied petroleum gas) stoves, refrigerators, and lamps.

Small hydroelectric plants are being installed in some rural communities. The flow of rivers and streams is measured, and where it is sufficient, waterwheels or turbines are erected. Eighty to 90 percent of controlled water energy can be used to generate electricity without producing waste residue or pollution.

Supplying electricity for large urban areas requires immense investments and construction. The Agno River in Mountain Province in northern Luzon was dammed in 1953. The giant Ambuklao Hydroelectric Plant there has a capacity of 75,000 kilowatts. Another hydroelectric plant on the Agno River was completed in 1960. A third plant, this one on the Angat River, supplies even more electricity and also water for irrigation, flood control, and for homes in the region north of Manila. Two more projects, the Masiway, completed in 1978, and the Magat River projects of 1983, supply electricity to the Luzon grid. Two new plants began operation on Leyte and Negros in July 1983.

INDUSTRY

To develop industrially, the Philippines must process more of its raw materials. Eleven major projects to achieve this are to be

...uburb of Manila built on marshlands

...mpleted by 1987. A large copper smelter and fabrication plant
...ll turn the ore into rods, wire, and other products. This will
...duce the amount of copper concentrates now exported.

...The projects are in varying stages of construction. They include
...integrated steel mill, an aluminum smelter, a petrochemical
...mplex, a pulp and paper mill, a diesel engine manufacturing
...nt, and heavy engineering industries. The expansion of the
...ment industry, coconut processing, and the manufacture of
...ogas will also increase productivity.

...New projects are planned for locales other than Manila.
...anufacturing now is heavily concentrated in the Manila area.
...ansportation, communication, and an adequate supply of
...ergy are considerations in locating the new factories.

...The country is not without industrialization at the present time.
...wever, production is centered on processing and assembly
...erations. Semiconductor devices head the list of products.
...xtiles, clothing, shoes, foods, beverages, tobacco, plywood,

A young Muslim girl (left) is weaving fabric and the young man (right) is making capiz shell pieces used in making lamp shades and wind chimes.

veneer, furniture, small appliances, and an automobile assembly plant are included in the industrial sector.

For many years clothing was made to measure. Now a wide variety of ready-to-wear apparel is available for the domestic consumer as well as for export.

The government is assigning high priority to the development of small and medium industries throughout the islands. They can provide employment and increased income to provinces now engaged only in agriculture.

COTTAGE INDUSTRIES

Cottage industries are the most widely dispersed of the country's manufacturing activities. There are two types. Household industries are usually operated by the members of a family. They produce handicrafts for domestic use and export. They process locally available materials, engaging in embroidery, od carving, brass work, abaca products, and capiz shell items. mall workshops are also considered cottage industries. They y manufacture textiles, process foods, or fabricate components electrical equipment.

he cottage industries export products to ninety countries. With ass market potential, these small rural industries add to usehold incomes in an economy being transformed from barter ash. They also reduce the pressure for migration to urban as in search of employment.

TOURISM

ourism contributes greatly to the Philippine economy. The nistry of Tourism actively promotes it as an industry. Over a llion visitors arrive annually, more than 25 percent from Japan almost 20 percent from the United States.

o boost earnings in foreign exchange, the ministry promotes rism in Japan, North America, Australia, and New Zealand, as ll as in Africa, Europe, and the Middle East.

he tourist industry provides jobs in many sectors. Benefits can found in the construction business, hotel and restaurant ilities, farming, handicrafts, and service industries. Twenty-ee airlines operate more than 150 flights weekly into Manila. ipinos say, "You've missed paradise if you haven't visited the ilippines."

CONSTRUCTION

Construction activity has been concentrated in urban areas, pecially in the Manila and central Luzon regions. Both the ivate sector and the government have contributed funds to

A primary school in a BLISS settlement

construct new buildings. Makati, with its new apartment buildings, hotels, offices, and condominiums, is one example of private enterprise involvement.

The BLISS program is a government project. The Bagong Lipunan (New Society) Improvement of Sites and Services (BLISS) project singles out depressed areas to set up model communities. A BLISS settlement includes housing, schools, health facilities, churches, marketplaces, and parks. Industry appropriate to the area is constructed to provide employment for the residents. By 1983 more than 80,000 families had benefited from the program in 1,500 communities.

Construction also has been evident in new airports, highways, port facilities, irrigation and water supply, power and rural electrification, and schools. Forty percent of the funding for these projects was obtained from foreign sources.

TRADE

Unfortunately, the country must import much more than it exports. Most of the ten principal exports are unprocessed or partially processed items. By 1981 semiconductor devices were t in export value. They were followed by sugar, coconut oil, ...pper concentrate, gold, lumber, bananas, iron ore concentrates, ...wood, and dessicated coconut.

Fuel oils and lubricants accounted for almost one third of the ...ports in dollar value. Machinery and materials for the ...nufacture of electrical equipment were second in import value. ...her major imports included appliances, explosives, equipment ...d accessories for all kinds of vehicles, textile fibers, chemicals, ...ins (especially wheat), cereals, dairy products, and computer ...tems.

The United States remains the country's major trading partner. ...e Philippines sells to the United States 30.9 percent of its total ...ort production and buys 22.9 percent of total imports. Japan ...ks second in foreign trade.

The countries in the Association of Southeast Asian Nations ...SEAN) account for about 40 percent of the trade. Hong Kong, ...stralia, South Korea, and New Zealand are also important.

The primary import from the Middle East is crude oil. Exports ...his area include portland cement, garments, fruits, and ...etables.

Countries in the European Economic Community purchase ...onut oil, handicraft items, forest products, garments, and ...niconductor devices. Trade with Socialist and Communist ...ntries, especially Russia and the People's Republic of China, ...vides the Philippines with a trade surplus. Nevertheless, the ...erall trade deficit in 1981 was almost $2.5 billion.

To compete favorably in world markets, the country must ...tall the most modern and efficient factories. Skilled workers ...st be employed. Markets must be found for finished products ...h at home and abroad.

Primary schoolchildren (above). Many village houses are still made
of bamboo sides and roofs of thatch or corrugated metal (below).

Chapter 10

LEARNING AND LEISURE

Filipinos have said that "the Spanish gave us our religion but the Americans gave us education." To a great extent that is true. The Filipinos have a high regard for education since it provides them with personal as well as family advancement.

PRE-HISPANIC EDUCATION

Before 1521 parents provided the initial education for their children. When they were older, boys were educated at the home of the leading elder in the village or barangay. The Filipinos had an alphabet of seventeen letters in a form of Sanskrit. They wrote on bark, bamboo, and leaves.

Little remains of pre-Hispanic writing. Leaves, bark, and bamboo have disintegrated. However, two legal codes from 1250 and 1433 have been found.

Folktales and epic poems were passed down orally from generation to generation in local languages. The Ifugao of Banaue in northern Luzon, for example, still recite or chant epic poems at ceremonies honoring the dead and at rice harvests. Traditional stories are told in many other regions, too. One tribe in northern Luzon has a myth about the repopulation of the world following a great flood.

EDUCATION UNDER THE SPANISH

The Spanish colonizers were anxious to spread their Christian faith. The old system of writing in Sanskrit was discouraged. Friars started small schools to teach Christian principles. The native languages were used since it was easier for one friar to learn the local language than for many villagers to learn Spanish. Relatively few Filipinos received instruction in these schools. Rarely were any students admitted to schools of higher education or taught Spanish.

Filipinos and mestizos (people of mixed Spanish and native parentage) who came from well-to-do families were able to send their children to secondary schools. Otherwise usually only the sons of Spanish families attended these private schools. Some young men were able to study at the Catholic universities. A few were able to continue their studies at universities in Europe, especially in Spain, and the United States.

EDUCATION UNDER THE AMERICANS

The Americans began a program of mass education after they occupied Manila in 1900. William Howard Taft, who was sent to the islands as a commissioner, ordered schools started within three weeks. The children were taught by American soldiers. Since few Americans knew Spanish or Tagalog, instruction was in English. Taft felt that the best way to prepare the Filipinos for self-government was through education. A common language, English, helped to unite people throughout the islands.

In southern Luzon near Legaspi, Captain Arlington Ulysses Betts decided to open a free school. In a short time Betts had established sixteen schools in the district.

In 1902 there were 1,074 American teachers. In 1910 there were 773, but there were also 8,275 Filipino teachers. In 1950 eight American teachers still remained, but the number of Filipino teachers had reached 85,396.

The University of Santo Tomas was founded in Manila in 1611 by the Dominican Archbishop Miguel Benavides. It was authorized to grant degrees in 1624. Until the late nineteenth century only students of Spanish parentage were admitted.

Santo Tomas became the internment camp for ten thousand American, British, Canadian, and other Allied prisoners held by the Japanese during World War II. Each day Filipinos sympathetic to the prisoners arrived at the fence around the campus. They passed small packages of food and supplies to the internees.

Children also were held in the Santo Tomas camp, along with many teachers. Classes for the children soon were organized, and continued despite the harsh conditions.

Filipino families are very close knit. The parents make every effort to educate the oldest child in the family. He or she, in turn, is expected to help sisters and brothers obtain an education.

PRESENT-DAY EDUCATION

Until recently primary (elementary) schools in urban areas offered six years of education, but rural schools only four years. Many schools now have added a seventh year, even in rural areas. Education is compulsory.

As a sense of nationalism grew, some people demanded that instruction in English be adandoned. They insisted that students be taught in Pilipino. (It is called "Pilipino" since there is no *f* in

The College of Education at the University of the Philippines

the Philippine language. However, the people are called "Filipinos," the *f* having been adopted by linguists who include Spanish and English words in Pilipino.)

President Marcos's Education Decree in 1972 returned English as a medium of instruction in the primary schools. Pilipino is taught as a subject in grades one through seven and in social studies instruction. English is taught in all seven grades and in science and mathematics classes. The local language is introduced in fourth or fifth grade.

About half of the nation's forty-two major universities are located in Manila. The University of the Philippines was opened in 1908. Its main campus is in Quezon City. The University of the Philippines at Los Banos teaches many disciplines, but its major emphasis is on agriculture and animal husbandry.

Baguio, Legaspi, Davao, and Cebu also have major universities. To curb the migration of rural students to the cities, thirty-nine community colleges have been opened. Over 650 institutions offer four-year programs in liberal arts or eight- and nine-year programs in medicine and law. Over one third of the college students study education. There is always a need for more graduates in agriculture and forestry.

In order to upgrade the quality of higher education, as well as to control college admissions, the National College Entrance Examination was instituted in 1973.

The Republic of the Philippines has the highest literacy rate in Southeast Asia. Nevertheless, it is estimated that 20 percent of the adult population has less than a year of education. Despite compulsory education and great efforts to provide educational opportunities for all children, many still do not attend. This is especially true in Muslim communities.

LEISURE

For most people, the most important religious and social occasion of the year is the feast day of their town's patron saint. Such fiestas are usually held after harvesttime. Houses are decorated with garlands of flowers. Relatives come from other islands to join in the celebration. The fiestas include religious rituals, a parade with the image of the saint carried through the town, a family feast, and all-night dance.

Christmas and Easter celebrations feature parades, processions, and religious observances. At the University of the Philippines students hold a candlelight lantern parade the week before Christmas.

In Muslim communities the first day of the tenth month of the Islamic lunar calendar is celebrated as New Year's Day. Games

On Marinduque Island (left) the Moriones hold a festival during Holy Week and in Cebu a family roasts a pig for a fiesta (right).

and sports, gift giving, and a musical performance are part of the observance. In June, Muslims celebrate the birthday of Muhammed. They also hold other religious festivals.

SPORTS

More and more Filipinos are becoming interested in competitive sports, especially basketball. Tennis, boxing, jai alai, swimming, volleyball, and baseball are also popular.

For several centuries cockfighting has been allowed on Sundays and holidays. Almost every town has its *galleria* where enthusiastic observers wager on the outcome. Cockfighting starts early in the morning and lasts until sunset.

Some popular sports in the Philippines are jai alai (above left), wind surfing (left), and cockfighting (above).

OTHER RECREATION

In urban areas many people visit museums and art galleries. Others engage in sailing or fishing or attend the many motion picture theaters. Unfortunately there are few libraries. In rural regions the local store may be the forum for men to debate political issues or the problems of the community.

Despite the drudgery of daily life, Filipinos are a happy and friendly people. They find pleasure in their extended families and may count as many as a hundred persons as relatives. Family gatherings celebrate almost any occasion—a baptism, a wedding anniversary, a promotion, a marriage, or a birthday.

The Theater for the Performing
Arts (above) in the Cultural Center in
Manila. An artist
carving jade horses (left)

Chapter 11

ARTISTIC EXPRESSION

The arts of the Philippines have been influenced by their Malay, Indonesian, Chinese, Spanish, and American contacts and heritage. The artistic expression in the culture of the Malay migrants served social and practical needs. The performing arts were used to pass on sacred beliefs. Practical arts provided the people with functional articles and clothing.

PRACTICAL ARTS

By 1000 B.C. the people on the islands were making jars for household use and for burials. Techniques were developed to make fabrics, jewelry, glass, and iron. Some of these crafts or the raw materials for making the items may have been learned from Chinese merchants.

Certain tree barks were pounded into a fibrous cloth called *tapa*. Tapa cloth was also made on other Pacific islands.

Weaving dates back to about 200 B.C. Traditional weavers on Mindanao and the Sulu Archipelago use yarns made from abaca and cotton. Abaca cloth is not as soft as cotton but acquires a sheen when "washed" in dry ashes. Then the cloth is rubbed with a piece of shell.

Traditional weaving is done on the backstrap loom. The weaver sits on the ground or a platform. Tension on the warp is controlled by leaning back on the backstrap. At the same time the weaver's feet are pressed against a piece of wood in front.

Other weavers use more modern forms of hand looms. It still takes many hours to complete enough material for a sarong or malong, a skirt worn by both men and women.

The Muslim religion permits only geometric designs. Vegetable dyes are used to color the thread or the finished product. Sulu Muslim men wear very tight trousers, while the women wear a loose-fitting type. Tube skirts are also worn by some Mindanao Muslim women. Both men and women wear handwoven shirts and blouses.

JEWELRY

When the Spaniards landed, they found important community leaders wearing gold jewelry. It is thought that gold artifacts found in burial sites were made in the Philippines, though the designs may have been influenced by contact with traders from Southeast Asian countries. Jade and glass jewelry also was found. Some of the raw materials for these items may have come from Chinese traders.

SCULPTURE

The early Filipinos believed in one great God known by a different name in each tribe. They made no images of their almighty God but did fashion images of lesser spirits. These were called *anitos*. These images were carved from stone, wood, gold, or

After an image is carved from wood, a finish is added to preserve it.

Chinese ivory. Following the Christianizing of the people, *santos*
replaced the anitos.

Santos are carved images of saints. Carvings are also made of
the Holy Family. Large santos are found in churches. Many homes
have small altars displaying a santo or a carving of the Madonna
or Christ.

By the time the Spaniards reached Laguna de Bay in 1571, Paete
was already a renowned wood-carving town. Wood carving is still
the main occupation of the men there. The women finish the
figures. Following their conversion to Christianity, Paete carvers
produced extremely fine santos. Some displayed during Holy
Week had movable parts manipulated by levers.

Churches were decorated with wood carvings over the altars
and on furniture. Stone carvings could be found on the exterior.
The churches had ornate interiors. Often the altars were gilded.

PAINTING

The earliest important painter was Damian Domingo. In 1826 he was appointed director of the first Academy of Drawing. It was founded in 1821 to teach students to draw and to paint in oil.

Lorenzo Guerrero is considered the first Filipino nonreligious painter of note. Other famous artists of the nineteenth and twentieth centuries include Simon Flores (religious); Filipe Roxas (landscapes); Juan Luna and Fabian de la Rosa (portraits); Felix Resurrecion Hidalgo, Carlos Francisco, and Vincente Manansala (murals); and Regino Garcia y Baza, Felix Martinez, Manuel Espiritu, Jorge Piñeda, and Fernando Amorsolo (illustrators). Other important artists are Diosdado Lorenzo, Victorio Edades, Galo Ocampo, Napoleon Abueva, and Ricarte Puruganan.

Paintings and sculptures are in great demand. Many galleries provide one-artist and group shows in Manila. To encourage participation in various art forms, the National Arts Center was opened on Mount Makiling near Los Banos in 1976. It has facilities for artists to live and work there, with classrooms, recreational facilities, an outdoor chapel, and a pavilion-auditorium seating 2,500. Those interested in music, dance, and drama also study at the Arts Center.

MUSIC, DANCE, AND DRAMA

Vocal music in the pre-Hispanic period consisted of songs of love, courtship, work, sacred ceremony, and humor, as well as funeral dirges. Many of these native songs are still sung, as are those in English and Spanish. Native instruments such as the bamboo flute and harp are similar to those developed in Malaysia.

Dancers performing the Tinikling dance

Gongs, bells, and a variety of stringed instruments are also played.

Dancers often sing or play instruments while they perform. Aspects of daily life are acted out in some dances. One of the most popular is "Planting Rice."

The Tinikling dance illustrates the movements of the Philippine rail, a small wading bird, as it runs between the grasses on riverbanks. Two people hold a pair of bamboo poles close to the ground. As they strike the poles together in rhythm another couple dances between and beside the poles. The dancers try not to have their ankles caught between the poles as the poles are moved faster and faster.

Many of the dances show both Muslim and Spanish influence. Muslim dances are performed in a stylized manner with almost no facial expression. Filipino dances, however, are expressive.

For a time it seemed that folk music and dances would be forgotten. Popular songs from the United States and Latin

America were widely played. In 1934, a committee from the University of the Philippines filmed and recorded some of the folk music and dances before they disappeared. The films were so enthusiastically received that the dances and songs were soon included even in classroom concerts.

The Bayanihan Dance Company performs traditional dances at home and on tours in foreign countries. The program includes early Malay, Muslim, and Spanish dances.

To encourage art, music, dance, and the theater, the Cultural Center of the Philippines was built on reclaimed land in Manila Bay. It was opened in 1969. It has a large concert hall, a smaller theater, museum, and art gallery. Both Filipino and foreign artists and performers are featured.

To help convert the people, the Spaniards introduced miracle plays depicting Bible stories. The *sinakulo*, performed during Holy Week, dramatizes scenes beginning with the Creation. Usually the sinakulo is a community project.

Filipino writers and composers wrote musical folk operas called *zarzuelas*. They were usually satires expressing social protests against the Spanish and Americans. Often the producers and authors were arrested.

In 1954 the Barangay Theater Guild was established. This company produced both radio and stage plays by Filipino writers, as well as new versions of English classics. Two famous playwrights are Nick Joaquin and Wilfrido Guerrero.

During martial law the theater productions changed. Writers and actors searched for national identity in traditional Philippine forms of the early twentieth century, although critics maintained these old forms were created in a social setting that no longer existed.

LITERATURE

The first Filipino literature consisted of oral poems. Most of the oral literature was derived from Hindu, Malayan, Muslim, and Chinese folktales. Ancient narrative poems have been preserved by the Sulu Muslims and people on Palawan, Mindanao, and the Ilocos regions.

The arrival of the Spanish stimulated a limited number of educated Filipinos to do some writing. Through the eighteenth century the most popular works were fantasies and legends of European origin.

By the middle of the nineteenth century the ilustrados (the enlightened ones) expressed their desire for freedom in poetic form. The foremost epic poem of this type was *Florante at Laura*, written by Francisco Balagtas in 1838. Jose Palma wrote *"Filipinas,"* a lyric poem that became the national anthem.

Jose P. Rizal was the most gifted writer in the late nineteenth century. While in Madrid in 1887, his first political novel, *Noli Me Tangere* (*The Lost Eden*), was completed. In his *El Filibusterismo* (*The Subversive*) he tried to show the Spanish their mistakes and injustices. He wrote many essays and poems.

Following the American occupation, Filipino writers continued to express their desire for freedom and nationalism in poetry and the *zarzuelas*.

Under President Quezon in the commonwealth period, literary competitions were held to stimulate the growth of national literature in English, Tagalog, and Spanish. Rafael Palma won the 1938 award for his biography of Jose Rizal. Originally written in Spanish, it was translated into English as *The Pride of the Malay Race.*

The influence of many cultures can be seen in the Muslim mosque (above left), the Chinese cemetery (above right), and the Christian church (below).

Chapter 12

THE PHILIPPINES IN THE COMPANY OF NATIONS

For centuries the Filipinos lived on their islands, accommodating each new wave of people landing on their shores. First a Malay heritage predominated. Then Arab traders, Indonesians, Chinese, Spaniards, British, Dutch, and Americans came. Finally, the Japanese occupied the islands during World War II. Each group left its own cultural marks upon the country. For most Filipinos their religion came from the Spanish. The Americans encouraged education and added a Western style democracy to the government. Finally, the Japanese offered independence within a shared prosperity sphere, but most Filipinos were not impressed.

The country's colonial period lasted for four centuries. With the interlocking influence of so many countries, the nation emerged visibly different from its neighbors in the Association of Southeast Asian Nations (ASEAN).

In 1935, when the country gained commonwealth status, a constitution similar to that of the United States was adopted.

Powers were divided among executive, legislative, and judicial branches of government. By 1940 the constitution was amended to provide for two houses in Congress instead of just one. This democratic form of government continued when independence was granted in 1946 and the Philippines became the first modern republic in Asia.

THE NEW NATION

Following World War II, Manuel Roxas, who had established the Liberal party, was elected the first president of the new republic. The date was July 4, 1946. Descendants of the ilustrados continued to influence political and economic affairs, providing both stability and resistance to change.

The problems facing the new nation were enormous. Manila had been leveled, public services were destroyed, food was scarce, inflation was high, and malaria returned after having been all but eradicated. During Roxas's administration the emphasis was on postwar rehabilitation.

When Roxas died in office, the vice-president, Elpidio Quirino, succeeded to the presidency. He was inaugurated in 1949 following election to a four-year term. Quirino instituted programs to improve social conditions. In 1949 he urged an Asian union based on common cultural, economic, political, and military bonds. When the United Nations was founded in 1945, the Philippines was one of the fifty original signers of the charter. Later, Carlos Romulo served as president of the General Assembly.

Unfortunately, Quirino's term was marked by corruption and violence. The growing militancy of the Huks further complicated plans for land reform. The Huks, a Communist group, had started as the People's Anti-Japanese Army in 1942, but by 1946 called themselves the People's Liberation Army.

The Huks terrorized the countryside. Quirino appointed Ramon Magsaysay as secretary of defense in 1950. Magsaysay's program was to build national confidence in the army. Soldiers were ordered to pay farmers for rice and chickens instead of just taking them. The army was also to be made combat effective. Magsaysay's plan worked. Many of the Huks surrendered and were resettled in Mindanao.

Ramon Magsaysay defeated Quirino in the 1953 election. As president he provided leadership in agrarian reform and self-government at the barrio level. He visited the provinces and was extremely popular.

In 1955 a new trade agreement with the United States was negotiated. Diplomatic relations with the Japanese were resumed when the Japanese agreed to pay war reparations. During Magsaysay's term the Southeast Asia Treaty Organization (SEATO) was formed to provide for regional defense.

Magsaysay was killed in an airplane crash at Cebu on March 17, 1957. His Malay features, modest rather than elite background, non-Spanish family name, and rural development programs had endeared him to the people he served.

Vice-president Carlos Garcia became president upon Magsaysay's death. He was elected to a full term in 1957. That year he signed into law a bill that outlawed the Communist party. Garcia's program stressed Filipino nationalism and economic independence. An agreement was reached with the United States whereby large land areas reserved for American military bases were released to the Philippine government.

Diosdado Macapagal, Garcia's vice-president, like Magsaysay

President Ferdinand Marcos

did not come from an elite family. Elected president in 1961, he announced objectives for his term in office: to restore economic stability, establish a base for future growth, and help the poorer citizens. He worked to abolish sharecropping by tenant farmers and eliminated some economic controls.

At first Macapagal's efforts to abolish sharecropping were encouraging, but by 1965 it was apparent the results were insignificant. In that year's election he failed in a bid for a second term. Instead, the electorate chose Ferdinand E. Marcos.

THE NEW SOCIETY

Ferdinand Marcos was a much-decorated guerrilla leader in World War II. When he assumed office he faced the same problems that had challenged his predecessors. The population was rapidly increasing. Agrarian reforms were essential. The industrial base required expansion. Migration to the cities from rural areas was causing problems with squatters, unemployment, and poverty.

On Mindanao the Muslims again were demanding separation. The New People's Army in central Luzon, a Communist allied group, directed armed opposition against the government. Although the NPA was small, with a membership of perhaps 1,200 and an additional 3,000 sympathizers, its guerrilla activities presented a major security problem.

In his bid for reelection in 1969, Marcos was challenged by Senator Sergio Osmeña, Jr.

Osmeña claimed that Marcos had failed to restore law and order, check corruption, cut unemployment, reduce poverty, and contain rising prices. The 1969 election was more violent than any other campaign, resulting in 107 killed and 117 wounded. But Marcos won, with 60 percent of the popular vote.

The political and economic life of the nation was still controlled by about four hundred elite families. Social and economic developments favored the privileged few instead of the impoverished majority.

Against this background, President Marcos knew the constitution prevented him from serving more than two terms. In March 1967, a bill was passed to establish a nonpartisan constitutional convention to frame a new constitution emphasizing greater sensitivity to the popular will.

The 312 delegates were elected in November 1970, and met in June 1971. Proposals were made to change the governmental structure. A parliamentary organization similiar to that of France and Great Britain was developed.

The convention approved the draft on November 29, 1972. The president, using powers assigned by the 1935 constitution, had placed the country under martial law in September 1972. He insisted martial law was necessary to prevent the violent overthrow of the government by Communist rebels. He claimed almost absolute power to implement reforms in economics, social, and political fields.

Under the new constitution the office of president would have been symbolic, with only ceremonial duties. A prime minister with full executive powers was to be the actual head of the government. Both officials were to be elected from the National Assembly by members of that body. Each term of office was to be six years. Reelection was prohibited. Legislative powers were to be held by the National Assembly, a unicameral (single lawmaking body) called the Batasang Pambansa.

Marcos's Proclamation 1081 decreed martial law on September 21, 1972. It was not announced until September 23. Before the decree was made public, several senators, congressmen, governors, and newspapermen were taken into custody. All but one newspaper, one television station, and four radio stations in Manila were closed. The president maintained that under martial law sweeping reforms could take place to restore law and order. Public rallies were forbidden. Curfew from midnight to 4 A.M. was enforced. Partisan politics were barred.

Marcos labeled his program the "New Society." He announced a land reform program. Changes in tax procedures and banking laws were made. Corrupt government officials were removed from office. The announced target was the oligarchic wealthy class, which had refused to surrender power in the past.

In general, the population agreed with the changes. Crime was reduced. Tax collection improved. The economy showed signs of recovery.

The president maintained that approval of the new constitution could not be obtained through popular vote. The people would

Malacanang Palace, the official residence of the president of the Philippines

need more time and education to make an intelligent choice. He arranged, therefore, for leaders in the barangays to attend a meeting at Malacanang Palace on January 17, 1973. The constitution was ratified by a show of hands.

On that same day the president signed two proclamations. One continued martial law. The other stated that an interim National Assembly would not yet be convened.

The powers of president and prime minister were combined by a constitutional amendment on October 20, 1972. President and Prime Minister Marcos was therefore in full control of the government. Another amendment provided that all decrees and presidential orders under martial law would remain the law of the land even after martial law was lifted.

A 1976 amendment provided for an interim Batasang Pambansa of no more than 120 members. The president was to convene the assembly, but instead continued to exercise legislative powers under martial law. Opposition leaders were sometimes accused of treason, for "destabilizing" the government, and imprisoned.

MARTIAL LAW LIFTED

Martial law formally ended on January 17, 1981, just before the arrival of Pope John Paul II. Following additional amendments in 1981, the constitution provided that the president would assume the powers of head of state and chief executive. The term of office would be six years.

In June 1981, President Marcos was elected to a six-year term, with the next election scheduled for 1987. Although he had been in office since 1965, it was expected that he would run for reelection in 1987. Should he be incapacitated or die in office, an executive committee of fifteen would govern the country until an election could be held. The president appointed his wife, Imelda Marcos, as a member of the committee. Many believe she might try someday to succeed her husband as chief executive.

Mrs. Marcos represents her husband at many international meetings. She holds the title of governor of metropolitan Manila and is secretary of human settlements.

The presidency could also pass to Cesar Virata, secretary of finance, chosen by Marcos in 1982 to serve as prime minister. The military are also interested in power.

OPPOSITION

The president is not without further opposition. Muslim uprisings continue in the south, with support from Libya and Saudi Arabia. Communist recruiters have had some success in rural areas. Unemployment has been estimated at 30 percent. A nationwide strike was threatened before Marcos left for his American visit. As a result, labor leaders were detained.

Sunset over Manila Bay

Senator Benigno Aquino was imprisoned under martial law. He was considered the leading moderate alternative to Marcos. In 1980 he was released to undergo heart surgery in the United States. He taught at Harvard University and Massachusetts Institute of Technology until 1983, when he announced his intended return to the Philippines. When he arrived at Manila Airport, he was assassinated. The first serious street demonstrations since 1972 resulted. Even businessmen joined in, when the value of their bank accounts abruptly declined. The opposition party warned the president that he had to choose between democracy and widespread revolution.

Governing a country scattered over such a large area of ocean presents seemingly insurmountable problems. Coupled with tremendous debt and international loans, the economy has faltered. Marcos's New Society must struggle to resolve many issues. How well he succeeds will determine his future in office and the welfare of his country.

MAP KEY

Lowercase letters refer to the insert

Agno	n12	Cordon	n13	Palapag	C7
Agoo	n13	Corregidor	o13	Palauig	o12
Agria Point	o13	Cotabato	D6	Palauig Point	o12
Alabat	o13	Culion	C6	Palawan	C5-D5
Alaminos	n12	Cuyo	C6	Panay	C6
Ambil	p13	Daet	o14	Panginay	o13
Anacuao	n13	Dagupan	n13	Paniqui	o13
Angadanan	n13	Davao	D7	Parcale	o14
Angeles	o13	Dinagat	C7-D7	Pasay	C6, o13
Aparri	B6	Dumaguete	D6	Pasig	o13
Arayat	o13	Dupax	n13	Patnanongan	o14
Atimonan	p13	Echague	n13	Perez	o13
Babuyan Islands	B6	Gapan	o13	Polillo	o13
Bacnotan	n13	General Tinio	o13	Polillo Islands	C6, o13-o14
Bacolod	C6	Gold	p13	Puerto Princesa	D5
Bacoor	o13	Guagua	o13	Quezon City	C6, o13
Bagabag	n13	Guimba	o13	Ragay	p14
Baguio	B6, n13	Gumaca	p14	Rosales	o13
Balabac	D5	Iba	o12	Rosario	p13
Balanga	o13	Ilagan	B6	Roxas	C6
Balaoan	n13	Iloilo	C6	Samar	C6-C7
Balayan	p13	Imus	o13	Sampaloc Point	o13
Bambang	n13	Infanta	o12, o13	San Antonio	o13
Bangued	B6	Jolo	D6	San Carlos	o13
Bani	n12	Jolo Group	D6	San Fabian	n13
Basco	A6	Jomalig	o14	San Fernando	B6, n13, o13
Basilan	D6	Jones	n13	San Ildefonso Peninsula	n14
Bataan	p13	Kalibo	C6	San Jose, Mindoro	C6
Bataan Peninsula	o13	Labo	o14	San Jose, Luzon (north)	o13
Batan Islands	A6	Lamitan	D6	San Jose, Luzon (east)	o13
Batangas	C6, p13	La Paz	o13	San Jose, Luzon (west)	o13
Bauan	p13	Larap	o14	San Juan, Luzon (north)	n13
Bauang	B6, n13	Legaspi	C6	San Juan, Luzon (south)	p13
Bayambang	o13	Lemery	p13	San Narciso	o13, p14
Bayombong	n13	Leyte	C6-C7	San Nicholas	o13
Binalonan	n13	Lingayen	B6, n13	San Nicolas	n13
Biñan	o13	Lipa	C6, p13	San Pablo	o13
Boac	C6	Laoag	B6	San Quintin	o13
Bohol	D6	Lobo	p13	Santiago	n13, n12
Bolinao	n12	Lopez	p14	Saragani Bay	D6
Botolan	o13	Lubang	p13, p14	Santa Cruz	o12, o13, p14
Bugsuk	D5	Lubang Island	C6	Santa Maria	o13
Burgos	n12	Lubao	o13	Silang	o13
Butuan	D7	Lucena	C6, p13	Solano	n13
Cabalete	o13	Luzon	B6-C6	Sorsogon	C6
Cabanatuan	o13	Macalelon	p14	Subic	o13
Cabarruyan	n12	Malaybalay	D7	Sulu Archipelago	D6
Cagayan	D6	Malolos	o13	Surigao	D7
Cagayan de Oro	D6	Mangatarem	o13	Taal	p13
Cagayan Sulu	D5	Manila	C6, o13	Tablas Nasbate	C6
Caiman Point	o12	Maricaban	p13	Tacloban	C6
Calaguas Island	o14	Mariveles	o13	Tagbilaran	D6
Calamba	o13	Masbate	C6	Tagaytay	o13
Calamian Group	C5-C6	Mauban	o13	Tagolo Point	D6
Calapan	C6	Mayon Volcano	C6, o13	Talaga	p13
Calauag	p14	Mindanao	D6-D7	Talim	o13
Calbalogan	C6	Mindoro	C6	Talisay	o14
Caloocan	o13	Mogpog	p13	Tanauan	o13
Camiling	o13	Morong	o13	Tanza	o13
Candelaria	o12	Mt. Apo	D6, D7	Tarigtig Point	n14
Canicanian	o14	Mt. Banahao	o13	Tarlac	C6, o13
Canlaon Volcano	C6	Mt. Halcon	C6	Tawi-Tawi	D5-D6
Cape Bolinao	n12	Mt. Labo	p14	Tawi-Tawi Group	D5-D6
Cape Engaño	B6	Mt. Malabito	o13	Taytay	C5
Cape Encanto	o13	Mt. Mantalingajan	D5	Tayug	n13
Cape San Agustin	D7	Mt. Pinatubo	o13	Tiaong	p13
Cape San Ildefonso	B6, n13	Mt. Pulog	n13	Tinaca Point	D7
Cape Santiago	p13	Muñoz	o13	Tonton	n13
Casiguran	n14	Naga	C6	Trece Martires	o13
Catanauan	p14	Naguilian	n13	Tuguegarao	B6
Catanduanes	C6	Naic	o13	Unisan	p14
Catbalogan	C6	Nasugbu	o13	Urdaneta	o13
Cavite	o13	Negros	D6	Verde	p13
Cebu	C6	Olongapo	o13	Victoria	o13
Cebu Island	C6	Orani	o13	Vigan	B6
Cervantes	B6	Orion	o13	Virac	n13
Cochinos Point	o13	Oroquieta	D6	Zamboanga	D6
Concepcion	o13	Ozamiz	D6		

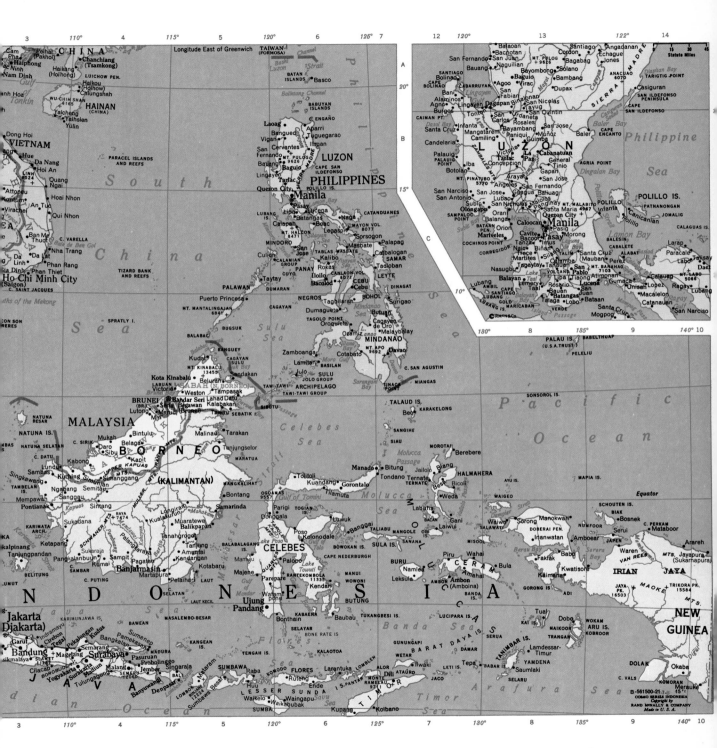

©Rand McNally & Co. R.L. 83-S-141

MINI-FACTS AT A GLANCE

GENERAL INFORMATION

Official Name: Republic of the Philippines (*Republika ng Pilipinas*)

Capital: Manila

Official Language: Pilipino (derived from Tagalog) and English

Other Languages: Eighty-seven different dialects and native languages

Government: The Philippines is governed by a constitution that was ratified in 1972 and proclaimed in effect in January 1973. However, President Ferdinand Marcos placed the country under martial law from September 1972, to January 1981, and governed under temporary provisions of the old constitution until his official election in 1981 to a six-year term.

Under the 1973 constitution, the prime minister was the head of government, while the president's position was supposed to be ceremonial. Both officials were to be elected from among the members of the National Assembly. The term of office was to be six years and reelection was prohibited. Legislative powers were to be held by the National Assembly, a unicameral (single lawmaking body) legislature called the *Batasang Pambansa*. But under amendments adopted in 1981, the president is the head of government and appoints the prime minister, who is to supervise the ministries (cabinet offices) and day-to-day legislative business. The president has broad powers and may be elected to an unlimited number of six-year terms. Regarding those powers, he or she can appoint the cabinet and dismiss members at will, declare martial law, and enter into treaties. The interim *Batasang Pambansa*, elected in 1978, theoretically has most of the same powers as the regular *Batasang* (scheduled to be elected in 1984), except for the power to ratify treaties.

Flag: Two horizontal bands—in peacetime, the top is blue and the bottom red; in war, the colors are reversed. They are joined at the left-hand end with a white triangle. Centered on the triangle is a yellow sun. In each corner of the triangle is a yellow star.

National Song: "Lupang Hinirang" ("Land That I Love")

Coat of Arms: The Filipino coat of arms bears Pilipino words meaning "one spirit, one nation." On it, the United States is symbolized by an eagle, Spain by a lion.

Religion: Eighty-three percent of the population is Roman Catholic; 9 percent is Protestant; 5 percent is Muslim; the remainder of the people living in remote mountain regions practice no established religion.

Money: The monetary unit is the peso. The exchange rate as of November 1983, was seventeen pesos to the dollar in United States currency.

Weights and Measures: The metric system

Population: 51,598,000 (1983 estimate). Distribution is approximately 64 percent rural, 36 percent urban. Density is 445 persons per sq. mi. (172 per km²).

Cities: The largest cities are:
Manila 1,330,788
Quezon City 754,452
Davao 482,233
Cebu 347,116
Zamboanga 261,978

GEOGRAPHY

Highest Point: Mount Apo, 9,692 ft. (2,954 m)

Coastline: The coastline of the more than seven thousand islands has a combined length of 10,000 mi. (16,090 km).

Mountains: The larger islands are mountainous. Mountains or hilly terrain make up 65 percent of the total land area.

Climate: The Philippines lies within the tropics. The climate in the lowlands is warm and humid. The average temperature is 60° F. (27° C) year-round. In the mountains it is much cooler.

On Luzon, the average annual rainfall ranges from 35 to 216 in. (89 to 549 cm) depending on the location. The wet season on Luzon in the Manila area lasts from June to November. In the cooler months, monsoon winds come from the northeast. From April to October the monsoons blow from the southwest. They carry heavy rains, especially from July through October. During these months, an average of twenty typhoons a year strike the islands.

Greatest Distances: The Philippines stretch 1,100 mi. (1,770 km) from north to south. They are 668 mi. (1,107 km) across at their widest part.

Area: The 7,107 islands of the Philippines are scattered over 500,000 sq. mi. (1,295,050 km²). If all the land surfaces were fitted together, they would occupy only 115,600 sq. mi. (299,416 km²).

NATURE

Trees and Flowers: More than ten thousand different species of flowering plants and ferns grow throughout the Philippine Islands. Over 40 percent of the land is covered with forest. Evergreen forests can be found in the lowland areas and up to 2,000 ft. (610 m) on mountains where there is sufficient rainfall. There, too, numerous native Philippine mahoganies grow to enormous size. Narra, the national tree, is a hardwood tree that grows in lowland rain forests. Mangrove trees grow along the coast and coconut trees are raised on plantations.

Fish: Over 750 species of saltwater fish are caught for food. The warm seas around the islands abound in fish, mollusks, and pearl oysters.

Animals: There are few wild animals in the Philippines. Monkeys, small deer, wild pigs, and some members of the cat family can be found in more remote areas. There are dozens of kinds of rodents and fifty species of bats. Crocodiles were once numerous throughout the islands, but now exist mainly in Mindanao. There are some poisonous snakes.

Birds: Almost eight hundred species of birds have been identified on the islands. Of these, one hundred species are migratory.

EVERYDAY LIFE

 Food: Filipino food bears the stamp of Malay, Chinese, Spanish, and American influence. Rice is the staple of the Filipino diet. Accompanying it often is some kind of seafood, such as crab, shrimp, and other shellfish. Fish is more often than not eaten marinated or roasted over coals. A popular dish is *sinigang,* which is sour fish soup.
Coconut is another common part of a Filipino meal. All parts of the fruit are eaten. Cooking meats and vegetables with coconut milk makes for hearty *guinatan.* Coconut (*niyog*) appears in salads, in the thick sweet called *macapuno,* and in other delicacies.
The Filipino national dish is *adobo,* usually a dark, saucy stew of chicken and pork, flavored with vinegar and soy sauce, garlic and liver bits.
Lechon, or Filipino roast pig, is usually served with an apple in its mouth. It is always provided at fiestas.
Fruit is very common in the Filipino diet, because it is so plentiful. There are mangoes, papayas, bananas of a dozen varieties, chicos, guavas, watermelons, and jackfruit, to mention a few.

Housing: In most rural areas, houses are still built as they were four hundred years ago. The huts, built of bamboo and wood, are raised above the ground on wooden pillars. They are roofed with nipa fronds from a type of palm. Nipa huts usually have only one or two rooms reached by a ladder. Except during rainy weather, cooking is done outdoors.
In Banaue, the rice terrace region of northern Luzon, the Ifugao build interesting nipa huts with large wooden washers on the bamboo pole supports. They prevent rats from climbing up. At night chickens are placed in wicker coops that hang from the floor.
In the cities, houses are built of more permanent materials, such as concrete blocks. The houses are much larger, too. Often they have lovely little gardens behind fences. The suburbs have their share of colonial or modern mansions. But not all people who live in the city live in comfort. Many who come from rural areas to seek a better life can't find work. These people often end up as squatters and build homes of scrap wood, sheet metal, and flattened cans or even cardboard.

Holidays: The Filipinos love holidays and festivals. Any excuse is good enough to hold a full-blown celebration. Patron saints, mythical figures, and historical events provide the inspiration. Because regional holidays and festivals are so numerous, the following list is of national holidays only:

New Year's Day, January 1
Holy Thursday
Good Friday
Bataan Day, April 9
Labor Day, May 1
Independence Day, June 12
Filipino-American Friendship Day, July 4
All Saints' Day, November 1
Bonifacio Day, November 30
Christmas Day, December 25
Rizal Day, December 30

Culture: The arts in the Philippines have been influenced by Malay, Indonesian, Chinese, Spanish, and American contacts and heritage. Artistic expression in the culture of the Malay migrants served social and practical needs. The performing arts were used to pass on sacred beliefs. Practical arts provided the people with functional articles such as clothing or jewelry. Filipino sculpture traditionally has had religious significance. The early inhabitants of the islands made *anitos,* images of their gods carved in stone, wood, gold, or Chinese ivory. After the Spaniards came, they carved *santos,* which were images of the saints or the Holy Family.

Painting is also very important in the Philippines. The first important painter was Damian Domingo, who lived in the early nineteenth century. Other famous artists of the nineteenth and twentieth centuries include Simon Flores, Felipe Roxas, Juan Luna, Fabian de la Rosa, Fernando Amorsolo, and Carlos Francisco.

Vocal music in the pre-Hispanic period consisted of songs of love and courtship, work, and religion. Many of these songs in native languages are still sung, as are those in English and Spanish.

Over the years Philippine music and dance have been influenced by the United States and Latin America. Yet efforts have been made during the past fifty years to foster Filipino culture also. To encourage art, music, dance, and the theater, the Cultural Center of the Philippines was opened in 1969. Both Filipino and foreign artists perform there.

The first literature consisted of poetry. Most of the oral literature was derived from Hindu, Malayan, Muslim, and Chinese folktales. In the eighteenth century, the most popular works by Filipinos were fantasies and legends of European origin.

In the nineteenth century, Filipino literature expressed social protest. For example, in 1887, Jose P. Rizal wrote the political novel *Noli Me Tangere* (*The Lost Eden*).

In the late twentieth century, Filipino literature has been influenced by martial law, which affected its quality and focus. Filipino authors would be more widely read in their own country if there were more libraries. Although libraries are found on college and university campuses, public libraries are rare.

Language: Tagalog

Kumusta po sila? How are you? *Magandang umaga po:* Good morning
Magandang hapon po: Good afternoon *Magandang gabi po:* Good evening

Sports and Recreation: More and more people are becoming interested in competitive sports. The most popular is basketball, followed by tennis, boxing, jai alai, swimming, volleyball, and baseball. Among water sports, scuba diving and snorkling have many fans.

Communications: Radio broadcasting in the Philippines began in 1922. At present, there are over 275 radio stations. However, many rural people cannot afford radios. There are 24 TV stations in the country. Through relay stations, television programs reach homes not only in Manila but in other urban areas.

Television series and movies from the United States are shown on Philippine stations. However, an increasing number of programs are being filmed in the Philippines. Many are educational series. Programs are in Pilipino as well as English.

At Baguio in the mountains north of Manila, the United States operates a relay station broadcasting news and cultural programs in English and eleven other languages. Included are programs of the Voice of America, which originate in Washington, D.C., and are sent by shortwave from the west coast of America to Baguio.

Following independence, Filipinos took great pride in their own free national press. The number and ownership of newspapers was limited during martial law. Although some newspapers resumed publication in 1981 in both English and Pilipino in Manila, the *Manila Times, Manila Chronicle,* and *Philippines Free Press* remained suspended. Many other cities and provinces have daily or weekly publications. Daily business newspapers and publications cover industrial and professional needs.

Transportation: Water is the most important mode of transportation in the Philippines. The national government operates 80 ports. Another 390 ports are under the jurisdiction of municipalities. There are 18 major ports and numerous minor ones. Besides inter-island ships, there is a lot of riverboat traffic. There are 2,001 mi. (3,219 km) of island waterways.

Highways connecting the islands are impossible to construct. Nevertheless, the most important road is the Pan-Philippine or Maharlika Highway. It goes for 1,250 mi. (2,011 km). Only 18 percent of the nation's roads are paved with concrete or asphalt. There were 94,965 mi. (152,800 km) of roads as of 1980. Of that, 12,430 mi. (20,000 km) were paved. The entire network of roads consisted of 71,300 mi. (114,722 km). A little more than 10,000 mi. (16,040 km) were paved.

Building and maintaining railroads on the islands are very costly. National railroads have been constructed only on Luzon and Panay.

Government-owned Philippine Air Lines (PAL) operates flights between Manila and cities in Europe, Asia, Australia, and the United States. There are five international airports.

Schools: The law requires children to attend school for at least six years. Until recently, primary schools in urban areas had six years of education and rural areas only four. As more money becomes available, many schools have added a seventh year.

President Marcos's Education Decree after imposing martial law in 1972 returned English as a medium of instruction in the primary schools. This was in spite of nationalistic fervor that condemned the use of English for a time. Pilipino is taught as a subject in grades one through seven and is the language of instruction for social studies. English is taught as a subject in all seven grades and is used in teaching science and mathematics. The regional language is introduced in the fourth or fifth grade.

About half of the forty-two major universities are located in Manila. The University of the Philippines was opened in 1908. Other cities, such as Baguio and Cebu, also have major universities. Recently, thirty-nine community colleges have been opened. Over 650 institutions offer four-year programs in liberal arts or eight- and nine-year programs in medicine and law. Over one third of the college students study education. There is always a need for more graduates in agriculture and forestry.

The Republic of the Philippines has the highest literacy rate in Southeast Asia. Nevertheless, it is estimated that 20 percent of the adult population has had less than a year of education.

Health: The health of the people of the Philippines is steadily improving. In the late 1970s, the death rate was only 10.3 per 1,000 persons. This improvement over earlier figures is particularly due to better care for expectant mothers and infants. Improved housing and pollution control, the provision of medical services to government employees, and the increasing number of nurses and doctors is expected to further extend the life of the average Filipino in coming years.

Principal Products:

Agriculture: Sugar, coconuts, rice, corn, pineapples, bananas, coffee, cocoa
Natural Resources: Timber, copper, nickel, iron, cobalt, silver, gold, chromite, mercury, zinc, lead, manganese, petroleum
Manufacturing: Textiles, pharmaceuticals, chemicals, wood products, food processing, electronics assembly

IMPORTANT PEOPLE

Emilio Aguinaldo (1869-1964), commander of Philippine rebel forces; president of the Malolos Republic, 1899-1901

Alexander VI (1431-1503), pope who assigned all past and future discoveries of land some distance west of Azores to Spain

Fernando Amorsolo, (1892-1972), illustrator

Benigno Aquino (1933-1983), leading opponent to President Ferdinand Marcos, assassinated at Manila airport

Francisco Balagtas (1788-1862) poet, author of *Florante at Laura*

Andres Bonifacio (1863-1897), revolutionary hero, founded the Katipunan, a secret society against the Spanish

Carlos Bulosan (1914-1956), World War II author

Andres Cristobal Cruz (1929-   ), post-World War II author

George Dewey (1837-1917), American naval commodore who commanded forces that secured the Philippines for the United States in Spanish-American War

Damian Domingo (1793?-1830?), first important painter

Sir Francis Drake (1540?-1596), English navigator and admiral who tried to take control of the Philippines

Victorio Edades (1895-   ), artist

Manuel Espiritu (1856-1921), artist

Simon Flores (1839-   ), religious painter

Carlos Francisco (1913-1969), mural painter

Carlos Garcia (1896-1971), president of the republic from 1957 to 1961

Regino Garcia y Baza (1840-1916), artist

N.V.M. Gonzalez (1915-   ), post-World War II author

Lorenzo Guerrero (1835-1904), first nonreligious painter of note

Francis B. Harrison (1873-1857), governor-general of the Philippines

Rajah Humabon (no record), native chief at the time Magellan landed

Nick Joaquin (1917-   ), post-World War II author

Lapu-lapu (1494-?), chief of the Mactan during the time of Magellan

Miguel Lopez de Legazpi (1510?-1572), first Spanish governor-general of the Philippines

Juan Luna (1857-1899), portrait painter

Diosdado Macapagal (1910-   ), president of the republic from 1961 to 1965

Douglas MacArthur (1880-1964), American general and leader of the armed forces in the Philippines during World War II

Ferdinand Magellan (1480?-1521), early European explorer, claimed the Philippines for Spain

Ramon Magsaysay (1907-1957), president of the republic from 1953 to 1957

Vincente Manansala, (1910-   ), mural painter

Ferdinand Marcos (1917-   ), present president of the Philippines republic

Imelda Marcos (1929-   ), member of the executive committee of the republic and wife of President Marcos

William McKinley (1843-1901), American president during Spanish-American War

Galo Ocampo (1913-   ), artist

Sergio Osmeña (1878-1961), president of the Philippine Commonwealth from 1944 to 1946

Jose Palma (1876-1903), poet who wrote "Filipinas," which later became the national anthem

Rafael Palma (1874-1939), biographer of Jose Rizal

Philip II (1527-1598), Spanish king for whom the Philippines is named

M.H. de la Pilar (1850-1896), revolutionary hero

Jorge Piñeda (1879-1946), illustrator

Manuel Quezon (1878-1944), first president of the Philippine Commonwealth

Elpidio Quirino (1890-1956), president of the Philippine Republic from 1948 to 1953

Claro Recto (1890-1960), playwright

Jose Rizal (1861-1896), author and patriot

Carlos P. Romulo (1899-   ), author who wrote of his experiences in World War II and present foreign minister

Manuel Roxas (1892-1948), president of the Philippine Republic from 1946 to 1948

Franklin Delano Roosevelt (1882-1945), American president during World War II

Jacob G. Schurman (1854-1942), first U.S. Philippine commission president (1899)

Rajah Sulayman (?-1571), native leader defeated by Legazpi in the sixteenth century

William Howard Taft (1857-1930), American president and commissioner of the Philippine Islands

Jose Garcia Villa (1908-   ), poet, author of *Have Come, Am Here*

Cesar Virata (1930-   ), present prime minister of the Philippines

Jonathan Wainwright (1883-1953), American general in the Philippines during World War II

Woodrow Wilson (1856-1924), American president

IMPORTANT DATES

C. 22,000 B.C.—Earliest known humans inhabit the Philippines

C. 900 A.D.—Beginning of trade with China

C. 1200—Islam spreads to the Philippines

1493—Pope Alexander VI decrees that all past and future discoveries some distance west of the Azores belong to Spain

1521—Ferdinand Magellan lands at Homonhon, is killed by natives

1565—Miguel Lopez de Legazpi arrives in Cebu, becomes first Spanish governor-general

1568—Portuguese fleet arrives to challenge Legazpi's territorial rights

1571 — Rajah Sulayman defeated by Legazpi; the city of Manila established

1577 — Sir Francis Drake of England lands at Mindanao

1592 — Construction of Fort Santiago begins

1609-1648 — Dutch blockade Manila harbor

1762 — English capture Manila

1763 — The Seven Years' War ends; Manila restored to Spain

1863 — Earthquake destroys governor-general's palace in Manila

1887 — Jose Rizal writes *Noli Me Tangere (The Lost Eden)*

1892 — The Katipunan, a secret political group in defiance of Spaniards, formed

1896 — Jose Rizal executed by Spaniards; Andres Bonifacio leads attack on Spaniards

1897 — General Emilio Aguinaldo elected president of revolutionary Malolos government; Aguinaldo signs pact with Spanish, expecting reforms; he and followers voluntarily go into exile in Hong Kong

1898 — Spanish-American War breaks out; Filipinos declare national independence; Treaty of Paris ending Spanish-American War gives the Philippines to the United States

1899 — Emilio Aguinaldo elected first president of Philippine Republic in spite of American claims to the territory; Philippine-American War begins

1901 — Philippine-American War ends; United States controls the Philippines

1916 — Jones Law promises eventual Philippine independence

1935 — Philippines gets commonwealth status; national elections held

1941 — Japanese attack Pearl Harbor and Manila

1942 — United States surrenders Philippines to the Japanese

1944 — General Douglas MacArthur returns to the Philippines

1945 — Japanese surrender to the United States; World War II ends

1946 — Philippines gains independence; Manuel Roxas becomes first president of the republic

1948—United States gets permission to establish memorial cemetery in the Philippines to honor Americans and Filipinos who died in World War II; President Manuel Roxas dies; Vice-president Elpidio Quirino assumes presidency

1949—Quirino elected to presidency; the Huks, a Communist group of former guerrillas, terrorize the countryside

1950—Ramon Magsaysay becomes secretary of defense and tries to build up the army

1953—Magsaysay elected president; Carlos P. Garcia becomes vice-president

1954—Philippines becomes charter member of SEATO (South East Asia Treaty Organization)

1955—New trade agreement negotiated with the United States

1957—President Magsaysay killed in airplane crash; Carlos P. Garcia elected president; Diosdado Macapagal elected vice-president; Communist party is outlawed

1961—Diosdado Macapagal elected president; Emmanuel Pelaez is vice-president

1962—President Macapagal moves Philippine Independence Day from July 4 to June 12, the date of General Aguinaldo's declaration of independence from Spain in 1898

1965—Ferdinand E. Marcos elected president; Fernando Lopez becomes vice-president

1969—President Marcos reelected

1972—Constitutional convention approves draft of new constitution providing for a parliamentary form of government; President Marcos declares martial law; powers of president and prime minister consolidated by constitutional amendment

1973—New constitution ratified, but rule by decree continues

1976—Constitutional amendment provides for interim *Batasang Pambansa* (National Assembly) of no more than 120 members

1981—Martial law ended; constitutional amendments establish president as chief executive; President Marcos elected to six-year term

1983—U.S. President Ronald Reagan and President Marcos agree on five-year military pact continuing lease on U.S. bases in the Philippines; opposition leader Benigno Aquino assassinated

Taal Lake

INDEX

Page numbers that appear in boldface type indicate illustrations

About the Author

Emilie Utteg Lepthien earned a BS and MA degree and a certificate in school administration from Northwestern University. She has worked as an upper grade science and social studies teacher supervisor and a principal of an elementary and upper grade center for twenty years. Ms. Lepthien also has written and narrated science and social studies scripts for the Radio Council of the Chicago Board of Education.

Ms. Lepthien was awarded the American Educator's Medal by Freedoms Foundation. She is a member of the Delta Kappa Gamma Society International, Chicago Principals Association and life member of the NEA. She has been a co-author of primary social studies texts for Rand, McNally and Co. and an educational consultant for Encyclopaedia Britannica Films. Ms. Lepthien has written another Enchantment of the World book on Australia.